The Collections of the Royal Geographical Society (with IBG) were used to research some of the details in this book. It is stimulating to see them used in such an inspirational way. The book should encourage children of all ages to find out more about the world they live in and how it is formed.

GEOGRAPHY HAS NEVER BEEN SUCH FUN BEFORE!

**Judith Mansell – Education Officer,
Royal Geographical Society**

Horrible Geography

PERISHING POLES

ANITA GANERI

Illustrated by
Mike Phillips

Hippo

Also available:

Violent Volcanoes

Odious Oceans

Stormy Weather

Raging Rivers

Desperate Deserts

Earth-shattering Earthquakes

Freaky Peaks

Bloomin' Rainforests

Scholastic Children's Books,
Commonwealth House, 1-19 New Oxford Street,
London WC1A 1NU, UK

A division of Scholastic Ltd
London ~ New York ~ Toronto ~ Sydney ~ Auckland
Mexico City ~ New Delhi ~ Hong Kong

Published in the UK by Scholastic Ltd, 2002

Text copyright © Anita Ganeri, 2002
Illustrations copyright © Mike Phillips, 2002

ISBN 0 439 99720 8

All rights reserved
Typeset by M Rules
Printed by Cox & Wyman

4 6 8 10 9 7 5

The right of Anita Ganeri and Mike Phillips to be identified as author and illustrator of this work
respectively has been asserted by them in accordance with the Copyright, Designs and
Patents Act, 1988.

CONTENTS

INTRODUCTION

Geography lessons. Snow laughing matter, are they? Some geography teachers freeze you to the spot with their brain-numbing knowledge of all kinds of weird words…

*Roughly translated, glaciation is the tricky technical term for how a place gets covered in ice. Gelifluction's the way frozen ground moves and sinks when the ice melts out of the soil in spring. Polynas are patches of water surrounded by sea ice. I bet you wish you'd never asked!

But chill out! It could be worse. Much worse. If you thought your classroom was horribly damp and chilly, thank your lucky stars you don't go to school at the f-f-freezing North or South Pole. You'd be so bloomin' busy keeping warm, you wouldn't have time to moan.

The bad news is that the parky Poles are the coldest, iciest and driest places on our whole perishing planet. They're also some of the windiest. And they're horribly far away. In fact, they're at the ends of the Earth and you can't get much further than that. Jolly good riddance, you might say. But you'd be wrong. The good news is that the perishing Poles are one of the most brilliant bits of geography ever. You'll soon be bitten by the polar bug (if the frostbite doesn't get you first).

Getting cold feet? Don't panic. The great thing about *Horrible Geography* is that you can visit far-flung places without having to leave home. This book is ideal for armchair travellers. Just like you. So find a comfy armchair, chill out and get stuck in. Just think how impressed your teacher will be with your new-found polar know-how. And you don't even need to pack an ice-pick.

If you're itching to know what it's really like at the Poles (without having to get up), try this simple experiment. Wait for a really cold winter's day. I'm talking the sort of day when you need a snow plough just to get out of your front door. The sort of day when going to school is COMPLETELY OUT OF THE QUESTION! Then send your little sister outside. (Call her in again after a few minutes. DON'T FORGET.) Look at your sister closely. Is she **a)** covered in goose pimples, **b)** frozen solid, or **c)** the proud owner of a blue nose?

If the answer is all of them, you'll have some idea of what it's like at the poles. (Don't worry – your sister won't be able to snitch. Her teeth will be chattering too much.)

And that's what this book is all about. Yes, colder than the coldest deepfreeze, and covered in ice several kilometres thick, the Poles are the coolest places on the planet. In *Perishing Poles*, you can…

• learn how to drive an Inuit dog sledge.
• search for deep-frozen mammoths buried under the ice.

IS THERE ANY POINT TO THIS?

- make a delicious dip from the contents of a caribou's stomach.
- track an iceberg the size of Belgium with ice-cool glaciologist*, Gloria.

* A glay-see-olo-gist is the posh name for a scientist who studies ice. Thank goodness someone knows what your teacher's wittering on about.

This is geography like never before. And it's horribly exciting. But be warned – wrap up warm before you start reading this book, even if you're staying indoors. You're about to embark on an icy adventure that'll send shivers down your spine.

RACE FOR THE POLE

1 November 1911, McMurdo Sound, Antarctica

In the perishing morning cold, the small team of men shook hands with their companions and said their goodbyes. Their mood was solemn. Would they ever see their friends again? No one knew. For they were about to embark on the biggest adventure of their lives. They were trying to become the first people to reach the South Pole, and earn a place in history. A horribly hazardous journey lay ahead of them across the icy Antarctic wastes. One man had seen it all before. Nine years earlier, expedition leader, Captain Robert Falcon Scott, had come within a few hundred kilometres of the Pole, before freezing cold weather and howling winds forced him back. This time steely Scott was determined to succeed, or die in the trying.

Preparations for the journey lasted almost a year. But on 1 June 1910, Scott's ship, *Terra Nova*, an old whaling ship which had been refitted and strengthened to break through the ice, finally left England. Six months later, after a stormy passage, *Terra Nova* moored in McMurdo Sound, among the drifting pack ice. Scott and his men built a hut on the beach at Cape Evans on Ross Island and settled in for the long, dark days of winter. (In the Southern Hemisphere, the seasons are the other way round. So from March to October, it's winter at the South Pole.)

Braving the treacherous temperatures, they busied themselves laying supplies on their route to the Pole and conducting scientific experiments. In the evenings, they listened to gramophone records and watched slide shows to help pass the time. So far, so good.

Now, at last, the waiting was over. The time had come to strike for the Pole. As he said his goodbyes, sombre Captain Scott looked cool and calm, but his thoughts were racing. He had left London safe in the knowledge that his greatest rival, the brilliant Norwegian explorer, Roald Amundsen, was at the other end of the Earth, heading for the Arctic. Amundsen was hoping to reach the North Pole first, leaving the South Pole to Scott. Or so he thought. On 6 April 1909, American Robert Peary claimed to have reached the North Pole, scuppering Amundsen's plans. Without telling anyone, ambitious Amundsen immediately changed course and headed south instead of north. The first thing Scott knew about it was a telegram from Amundsen which read:

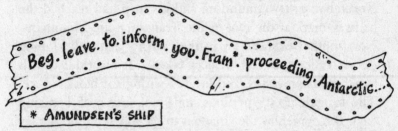

Beg. leave. to. inform. you. Fram*. proceeding. Antarctic...

* AMUNDSEN'S SHIP

But by that time, Amundsen was already on his way. There was no turning back for either of them. The race for the South Pole was well and truly on. Ten days after Scott's arrival, Amundsen and his party landed at the Bay of Whales, on the Ross Ice Shelf, and set up their camp (called Framheim). Everything had gone according to plan. While Scott and his men were saying goodbye, Amundsen was already well under way.

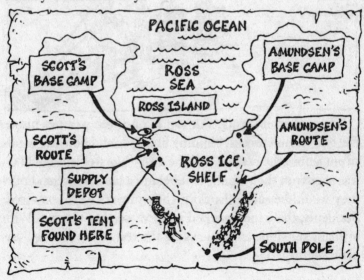

December 1911/January 1912

By the time Scott left Cape Evans, Amundsen was 12 days in front of him. And his lead was lengthening. By 17 November, gritty Amundsen and his men had reached the halfway mark at the foot of the Transantarctic Mountains. Now another obstacle lay in their path – a steeply sloping glacier, called the Axel Heiberg Glacier. It was riddled with treacherous crevasses, and littered with giant blocks of ice. The struggle up the perilous slope took four back-breaking days. But somehow they made it to the top. Now all that lay between them and the Pole was a vast expanse of dazzling white ice (called the polar plateau), stretching as far as the eye could see.

Then disaster struck. Almost at once the weather broke. For two terrible weeks, blinding blizzards and howling winds swept across the plateau. All the gutsy Norwegians could do was shelter in their flimsy tent behind a block of ice and pray they would be saved. Luckily, their prayers were answered. Suddenly, the wind dropped and the weather cleared. With brilliant sunshine and blue skies, the rest of the journey was plain sailing.

On 14 December, Amundsen and his hardy companions stood at last at the South Pole. Without a word, the men shook hands. There was no need to say anything. They'd made it – that was enough. But they did not dare stay very long. As they knew to their cost, the weather could change at any time. Amundsen spent three days fixing his position accurately, using a sextant (that's an old-fashioned instrument for navigating by measuring the angle between the horizon and the sun) to prove to everybody he had really made it. Before leaving, the men pitched a tent and planted a Norwegian flag on top. Amundsen also left a note for Scott, asking him to forward news of their triumph to the king of Norway. The note read:

Dear Captain Scott,

As you probably are the first to reach this area after us, I will ask you kindly to forward this letter to King Haakon VII. If you can use any of the articles left in the tent, please do not hesitate to do so. With kind regards.
I wish you a safe return.
Yours truly, Roald Amundsen

Six weeks later, the Norwegians returned to Framheim, fighting fit and well. They had completed their epic 2,500-kilometre journey in a staggering 98 days.

Meanwhile, Scott was in desperate trouble. As Amundsen proudly posed for photos at the South Pole, Scott and his men were struggling up another treacherous glacier, called the Beardmore Glacier, almost 640 kilometres away. Finally, on New Year's Day 1912, they too reached the polar plateau. Now, at last, the end was in sight and their spirits rose. Little did they know that Amundsen was already on his way home. For his final strike on the Pole, Scott picked four trusty companions – Edgar Evans, Lawrence Oates, Henry Bowers and Dr Edward Wilson. The rest of the support team was sent back. It was a superhuman effort. With temperatures plunging below an icy -40°C, every step was agony.

But worse was to come. On 16 January, the men spotted a black flag in the distance. And it seemed to be marking a camp. Amundsen had beaten them to it. Their worst fears had come true. In his diary, Scott summed up their dashed dreams:

"The worst has happened, or nearly the worst... The Norwegians have forestalled us and are the first to the Pole. It is a terrible disappointment... Tomorrow we must march on to the Pole and then hasten home with all the speed we can compass."

Bitterly disappointed, Scott reached the Pole two days later.

"Great God!" he wrote in his diary. "This is an awful place."

The return journey

Exhausted, starving, suffering from frostbite and with their spirits broken, Scott and his men began their nightmare journey home. Drifting snow covered their tracks and they frequently lost their way. One by one, the men's strength began to fail. On 17 February, Edgar Evans died after a fall into a crevasse. A month later, brave Lawrence Oates walked out of the tent into a blizzard. "I am just going outside," he said. "And may be some time." It was the last time they saw Oates alive. His feet were so badly frostbitten that he preferred to die alone rather than slow his companions down.

On 19 March, with food and fuel rations running dangerously low, the three survivors, Scott, Wilson and Bowers, found themselves trapped in their tent by a blinding blizzard. Howling gales and whirling snow made it impossible to battle on. Just 18 kilometres away lay a supply depot stocked with food and fuel that would have saved their lives. But it remained tantalizingly out of reach. For days, the men waited for the weather to clear but they knew in their hearts they were doomed. Each day, they grew weaker. With the last of his strength, Scott wrote letters home and kept up his diary. The last entry was dated Thursday, 29 March 1912. He wrote:

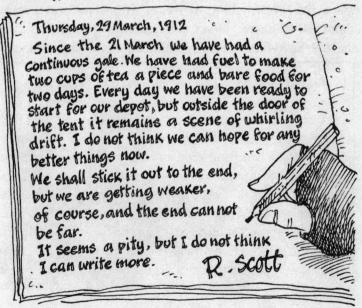

Thursday, 29 March, 1912

Since the 21 March we have had a continuous gale. We have had fuel to make two cups of tea a piece and bare food for two days. Every day we have been ready to start for our depot, but outside the door of the tent it remains a scene of whirling drift. I do not think we can hope for any better things now.

We shall stick it out to the end, but we are getting weaker, of course, and the end cannot be far.

It seems a pity, but I do not think I can write more.

R. Scott

The following November, a search party found the snow-covered tent, and the three bodies inside it. Scott's diary and letters lay beside him. A snow cairn with a cross made from skis was built over the spot.

Five frostbitten reasons why Amundsen reached the South Pole first

1 He had a head start. Amundsen pitched camp right at the edge of the Ross Ice Shelf – a pretty risky thing to do. If the ice had broken off, his camp would have drifted out to sea. But it was a risk worth taking. It meant Amundsen was already about 100 kilometres closer to the South Pole than Scott. By the time Scott finally set off, Amundsen was a long way ahead.

18

2 He let husky dogs do all the hard work. They were fast, well trained and tough. Six top-notch dogs could pull a half-tonne sledge up to 100 kilometres a day. At first, the men rode on the sledges, then were pulled along on skis. Scott had little experience of using dogs. He also thought it was manlier for his men to pull the sledges themselves, even though it was back-breaking work. One man wrote that it felt like his insides were being jerked out. The going was too tough for the ponies Scott brought all the way from Siberia. The poor beasts sank up to their knees in the snow and their sweat froze on their fur. To put them out of their misery, the ponies were eventually shot. As for the expedition's three motorized sledges – two broke down and one was dropped overboard as it was being unloaded.

3 His men ate fresh meat. Amundsen knew that without supplies of fresh meat his men would die of scurvy (that's a deadly disease caused by a lack of vital vitamin C). So when supplies ran out, he did the dirty on the dogs. At a place called "The Butcher's Shop", on the polar plateau, he had half the dogs (over 30) shot dead. Some of them ended up as dog-meat, while the men had fresh dog cutlets for dinner. Squeamish Scott thought eating dogs was horribly cruel. His staple diet was pemmican (a ghastly mixture of dried beef

19

and lard) and oatmeal porridge with the odd penguin or seal steak thrown in. Trouble was, pulling sledges used up loads of energy and there wasn't enough to eat. While Amundsen's team was well fed from the start, Scott's men ran out of vitamins and slowly starved to death.

4 He studied the Inuit people. Amundsen had learned crucial lessons from the local Arctic people about surviving the teeth-chattering cold. He had his clothes made from wolfskin, following an Inuit design. They kept the men warm and dry, even when temperatures plunged below -40°C. Scott, on the other hand, preferred clothes made from cotton and wool. The snag was they weren't warm enough and didn't allow sweat to escape. So the men ended up freezing cold *and* sopping wet.

AT LEAST THEY COULD HAVE TAKEN THE TEETH OUT!

5 He wasn't bothered about science. Amundsen's aim was simply to reach the South Pole. So he hand-picked a team of top polar experts for the gruelling journey. They included expert dog handlers and sledge drivers, and a super-fit ski champion. Amundsen himself began to train as a doctor but gave it up to explore instead. (As a kid in Norway, he'd dreamed of reaching the South Pole. He even slept with his windows open in winter to toughen himself up for the trip.) Scott, meanwhile, was dead keen on science. He loaded his sledges with heavy rock samples which made them horribly hard to pull. (Actually, the rocks turned out to be crucial clues and showed Antarctica used to be much warmer than it is today. Sadly, this startling discovery came too late for poor Scott.)

6 He had all the luck. On his return journey Scott was faced with freak cold weather. Instead of the usual temperatures of -30°C, Scott had to cope with temperatures which plunged below -40°C. Meanwhile, Amundsen was safely back at base.

It's a fact, then. The Poles are perilous places to be. As plucky Captain Scott found out to his peril, you need to be horribly tough to survive in the bitter cold. Think *you* could take them on and still come out alive? First you'll need to get to know the Poles better. A lot better…

THE PARKY POLES

Imagine miles and miles of ice and snow, as far as the eye can see. Add some battering blasts of wind, and some freezing cold temperatures. It's like peeking inside the biggest, coldest deep freezer on Earth – but without the frozen chips and ice lollies. Welcome to the parky Poles.

Pole position

Forget maypoles, flag-poles and tent poles, these aren't that sort of pole. No, they're actually the very ends of the Earth, at either end of the Earth's axis (that's an imaginary line running down its middle). This means you can only go south from the North Pole, and from the South Pole everywhere is north. Confused? Don't be. Here's Gloria with handy polar diagram no. 1.

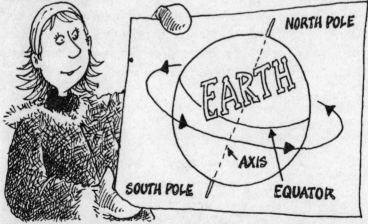

To muddle matters more, horrible geographers call the regions that surround the North Pole the Arctic, and the regions that surround the South Pole the Antarctic or Antarctica. Together they cover a chilly eight per cent of the Earth's surface.

Time for handy polar diagram no. 2.

But you can't blame horrible geographers. Oddly enough, it was the ancient Greeks who first thought up the names. Bet you didn't know that "Arctic" comes from the Greek word for, er, bear? Only this polar bear wasn't white and furry. And it didn't hunt seals on the ice. No, this was a bear-shaped pattern of stars that shone over the North Pole. And "Antarctic" simply means opposite the bear.

Actually, the globe-trotting Greeks never went near the Antarctic so how on Earth did they know it was there? The terrible truth is, they didn't. It was all down to guesswork, and the Greeks were brilliant at that. They reckoned there must be a lump of land at the bottom of the world to balance out the lump at the top. Otherwise, the top-heavy Earth would topple over. Incredibly, they were right – but not about the Earth toppling over. Antarctica really does exist.

Poles apart

You might think both parky Poles look much the same. I mean they're both freezing cold and icy, right? But actually, beneath their icy exterior, the Poles are worlds apart. So how on Earth do you tell which Pole is which? Getting your Poles in a puzzle? Not sure which end of the Earth you're at? Why not try this ice-cold quiz to tell the perishing Poles apart. All you have to do is answer NORTH POLE, SOUTH POLE or BOTH to each question. Ready?

1 It's a continent covered with ice.
2 It's a piece of frozen ocean.
3 There are polar bears but no penguins.
4 In summer, the sun shines all night.
5 In June, it's the middle of winter.
6 People live here all year round.

Answers:

1 SOUTH POLE. Underneath all that ice, there's a colossal continent lurking. Antarctica covers 14 million square kilometres – that's almost twice the size of Europe. But 99 per cent of it is capped by a gigantic sheet of ice, nearly 5 KILOMETRES THICK in places. That's enough to reach halfway up mighty Mount Everest. The ice is so bloomin' heavy, the land's sunk beneath its weight. And that's not all. Buried beneath the awesome ice are massive mountains and violent volcanoes. Luckily,

---

24

most of them are extinct – but one freaky peak, Mount Erebus, could blow its top at any time.

Antarctica's completely surrounded by the Southern Ocean. In winter, around a third of the ocean freezes over, increasing Antarctica's size. **Warning**: don't fall overboard when you're on your next polar expedition. This stormy sea's so perishing cold your brain would freeze solid in a matter of minutes. Brrrr!

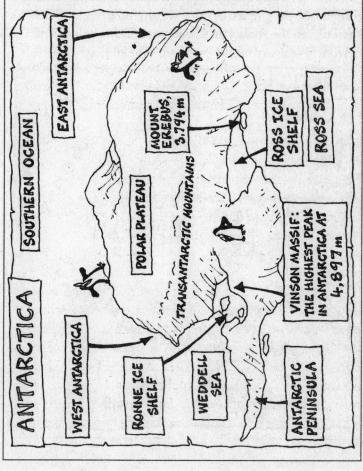

2 NORTH POLE. There isn't any land at the North Pole, only frozen ocean. The Arctic Ocean's the world's smallest ocean (it covers 14,000,000 square kilometres), and the chilliest (watch out, brain!). For most of the year, it's covered in drifting ice up to 3 metres thick. The Arctic Ocean's almost entirely surrounded by land. This includes the northern parts of Canada, Alaska, Scandinavia and Russia, together with glacial Greenland. Together they make up the region geographers call the Arctic. So the Antarctic's land surrounded by sea, and the Arctic's sea surrounded by land. Got all that?

3 NORTH POLE. There are no penguins at the North Pole. You might bump into a polar bear but if a penguin pootles past you, you're at the wrong perishing Pole!

ARE YOU SURE I'M LOST?   TRUST ME!

4 BOTH. If you can't get to sleep... (so no change there, then). The Sun doesn't rise for weeks on end and it's dark all the time. At the South Pole in winter, it's dark for six months on end. Why on Earth does this happen? Well, as the Earth orbits (circles round) the sun, it spins once on its axis, every 24 hours. The Earth's axis also tilts over at an angle. This means that some places on Earth tilt towards the sun and others tilt away, so some places have longer hours of daylight. This is why the length of the days and nights changes throughout the year.

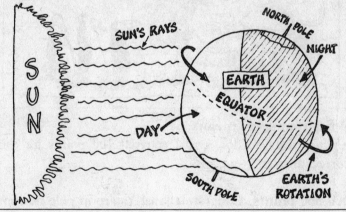

5 SOUTH POLE. While you're lazing about on the beach during your summer holidays, it's winter at the South Pole. And when it's winter in the north, it's summer down south. If you see what I mean. This is because, in June, the northern hemisphere tilts towards the sun and has summer. But the southern hemisphere tilts away from the sun and has winter. And in December, you get the reverse.

6 BOTH. Local people have lived in the Arctic for years and years. And they're experts at surviving. (You can meet some of them in **Perishing Polar People**.) But it's a different story at the South Pole. Only a few horribly hardy scientists live there all year round. It's just too bloomin' cold. And they're a very long way from home. Your nearest neighbours live in South America, about 3,000 kilometres away. Never mind, you'll have millions of penguins to keep you company.

WOTCHA!

What your score means...

So how did you do? Award yourself 100 points for each correct answer.

500-600 points. Congratulations! You're in pole position. But don't get carried away. Next thing you'll be suggesting a

perilous polar field trip to your teacher. Perish the thought.
300–400 points. Not bad. You're obviously warming to your
subject. But be careful – you could still slip up on the ice.
200 points and below. Terrible. You're really skating on
thin ice. You'll never be a geographical genius at this rate.
But if you really can't tell your Poles apart, here's a simple
diagram to help. You'll need to turn the book upside-down to
spot the South Pole, or stand on your head…

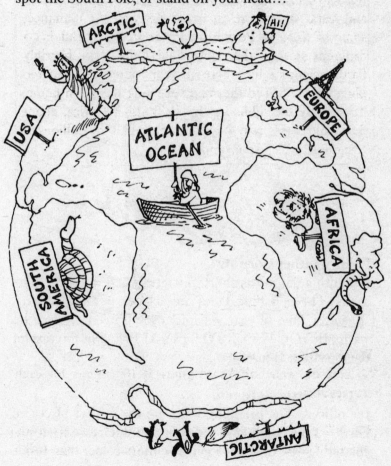

Polar weather report

Planning a personal polar expedition? Best check out Gloria's perishing polar weather forecast before you venture out...

Today will start off bitterly cold with temperatures well below freezing. Expect gale-force winds in the afternoon with the likelihood of a blizzard. And watch your step in winter, it will be pitch black all day. Tomorrow will be much the same, and the next day, and the day after. Summer might be a bit warmer (if you can last out that long, and at least you'll be able to see where you're going).

Polar weather warning

If you thought it was chilly in winter where you live, think again. The perishing Poles are absolutely f-f-f-freezing. Whatever time of year you pick, you'll need to wrap up warm. IF YOU WANT TO STAY ALIVE. The forecast for the forseeable future is:

Teeth-chatteringly cold

It's official. The perishing Poles are the coldest places on Earth. At the South Pole, the average temperature is a teeth-chattering -49°C, that's about five times colder than inside your freezer. But quite toasty compared to a place called Vostok where temperatures plummet as low as -89°C. Now that's plenty cold enough to freeze you to death. It's a lot warmer at the nippy North Pole, a toasty 0°C in mid summer (though it's -30°C in winter). But why on Earth are the Poles so bone-chillingly cold? Sorry, horrible science lesson alert… It's because the Earth's surface curves and so the sun's rays hit the Poles at a wide angle. They spread out over a wide area, which makes them weaker. The sun's rays also have to take a longer path through the Earth's atmosphere to reach the Poles. So some heat's soaked up or scattered by the atmosphere before it even hits the ground.

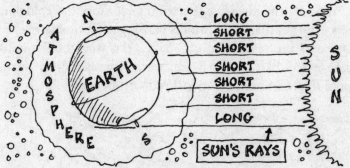

What's more, most of the sunlight that strikes the Poles is reflected straight back by the white ice. Horrible geographers call this the albedo effect. Put simply, it means that dark colours soak up heat while white reflects heat away. And it's why wearing a white T-shirt on a hot day keeps you cooler than wearing a black one. Try it for yourself and see.

Wild and windy

Watch out for wind at the perishing Poles. Seal steaks can play havoc with your insides. (Only joking. It's not that sort of wind.) This sort of wind can howl down the icy slopes at a staggering 200 kilometres per hour, as fast as a train. Fast enough to knock you off your feet. Or batter you with a blinding blizzard. A blizzard's a savage snow storm whipped up by the wind. Woe betide you if you're caught up in one. It'll blast snow into your mouth so you can't breathe, and make it impossible to see. And it's one of the main reasons polar explorers get hopelessly lost, often with tragic results. Worse still, the wind makes it feel far chillier than it actually is. You see, the stronger the wind's blowing, the colder it feels. And get this. If the wind's blowing at 50 kilometres per hour and the temperature's -35°C, the wind chill would make it feel like -80°C. If you weren't wrapped up warm you'd freeze solid in seconds. Pretty grim, really...

Dry as a bone

Strictly speaking, geographers count the South Pole as a desert. No, their brains haven't turned into icicles. This isn't the sort of desert you're thinking of, with sizzling sand

32

dunes, palm trees and camels. But it's a desert all the same. Geographers describe a desert as a place which gets less than 250 millimetres of rain or snow each year. And Antarctica gets only a fifth of that. Even though it's covered in frozen water,

parts of Antarctica are even drier than the bone-dry Sahara Desert. In some places, such as the dry valleys near McMurdo Sound, no rain has fallen for two million years.

Earth-shattering fact
The perishing South Pole was once warm and tropical. Believe it or not. Scientists found fossils of the same plants and animals in ancient rocks from Australia, South America and Antarctica. They showed that 200 million years ago these continents were joined together. Amazingly, Antarctica was covered in lush, green forests where dinosaurs roamed about. Then, about 180 million years ago, the three continents split apart and became separated by sea. South America and Australia stayed toasty warm. But Antarctica drifted to the South Pole and got colder and icier.

Awesome aurorae

If you're out and about during the long winter nights at the North Pole, and you suddenly see bright, flashing lights in the sky – DON'T PANIC. It isn't an alien spaceship on a mission to abduct your teacher (you wish). No, this spectacular polar light show is called the aurora borealis*. It happens when electrical particles stream from the sun and bash into gases in the Earth's atmosphere. Oh, so you knew that already? Well, in the past people hadn't a clue what caused the awesome aurorae. So they made up stories to make sense of what was going on.

> * Roughly translated, aurora borealis means "northern lights". Aurora's the old Roman name for the goddess of dawn and borealis means northern. At the South Pole, you get southern lights, or aurora australis.

WICKED!

1 The Inuit people of Canada thought the sky was a dome stretched over the Earth. Holes in the dome let light in and the spirits of dead people out. They believed the aurorae were blazing torches that guided the spirits to heaven.

2 The Vikings believed the northern lights were the breath of heavenly warriors. When they died, they fought out battles for ever in the sky.

3 Other people found the lights frightening. They thought (wrongly) that they spread death, disease and war. It was best not to mess with them in case they turned nasty. This meant not waving, whistling or staring. Else they might reach down and grab you. Bet you're scared.

A mammoth discovery

Warning: while you're busy ogling the aurora, watch your step. You might be about to stumble on a truly gigantic, and I mean mammoth, surprise. You might not know this but hundreds of prehistoric woolly mammoths (like enormous hairy elephants) have been found deep-frozen in the rock-hard Siberian ground. (It's so bone-chillingly cold the ground never thaws out so it's known as permafrost.) They've been buried for thousands of years since before the last Ice Age. Some are so well preserved you can still see their shaggy, red hair, and even cook and eat them. At a banquet in Russia in the 19th century, defrosted mammoth steak was the dish of the day. Fancy a mouldy mouthful?

NOT MAMMOTH AGAIN?

There's just one tiny problem – before you can tuck into your monster dinner, you'll have to defrost it first. Here's how to do it.

A mammoth task
What you need:
- A deep-frozen mammoth, about 20,000 years old
- Some tools – shovels, pickaxes, drills and jackhammers
- A helicopter
- Lots of hair-driers
- A large oven and deepfreeze
- A gas mask

What you do:

1 First, find your mammoth. But wrap up warm – snowbound Siberia's the best place to look for this beast.

2 Dig up the mammoth. This might be easier said than done. The frozen ground's as hard as concrete, but your jackhammer should do the job.

3 Lift the mammoth out of the ground. You'll need the helicopter for this bit. Make sure it's tied on tight – this unusual ice cube weighs a mammoth 20 tonnes.

4 Choose a nice, cold place to keep your mammoth, like a massive deepfreeze or an ice cave. That way, it won't melt and go mouldy as you chip the ice away.

5 Defrost the mammoth with the hair-driers. But be warned. This is a horribly tedious task and could take you months or years. (Never mind. Think of all those ghastly geography lessons you're going to have to miss. And you'll need your gas mask as your mammoth defrosts. It'll make a terrible pong.)

6 For a roast dinner with a difference, cook your mammoth in a giant oven (cooking time: one week). Then serve it up with some veg and gravy, and add tusks to decorate. Simple!

Before you rush off to recover from your mammoth tusk, sorry, task, here's a quick question. What's cold, white and slippery? No, it isn't disgusting school dinner rice pudding. Give up? Well, without it, glaciologists like Gloria would have to look for another job. What is it? Ice, of course.

Some people think ice is boring. I mean, apart from deep-freezing mammoths and cooling down drinks, what on Earth is frozen water good for? It's about as much use as a chocolate teapot. But not as tasty. But there's much more to ice than meets the ice, sorry, eyes, as you're about to find out.

Could you be a glaciologist?
Some horrible geographers like Gloria spend their whole lives studying ice. What d'ya mean, you'd rather watch a mammoth defrost? Could you be a cool glaciologist? If you think one lump of ice looks just like another, you'd better dip into Gloria's *Which Ice?* guide and get to grips with the different ice types.

Which Ice?

Ice sheet
Description: A vast sheet of ice that covers Antarctica and Greenland.
How it forms: From snowflakes which fall on the ground and get squashed by more snow falling on top. Slowly, air gets squeezed out of the snow and it turns into ice. But it takes thousands and thousands of years.

Got some spare time on your hands? Why not make your own ice sheet? All you have to do is make a few ice cubes – about 1,000 MILLION MILLION MILLION should do. That's how much ice is frozen in the awesome Antarctic ice sheet. Oh, by the way, you'll need a deepfreeze twice the size of Australia to keep your ice sheet in.

Glacier
Description: A gigantic river of ice.
How it forms: From ice that flows from the centre of an ice sheet. To look at, an ice sheet seems horribly solid. But oddly, the ice is like runny icing on a birthday cake. It flows out from the middle of the sheet and moves slowly towards the sea. The record-breaking Lambert Glacier in Antarctica is a staggering 515 kilometres long and over 40 kilometres wide. That's one big birthday cake. Luckily, this gigantic glacier creeps along at a snail's pace, at about 2.5 centimetres a day.

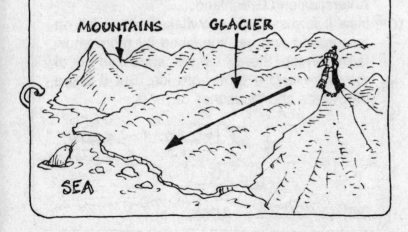

MOUNTAINS   GLACIER

SEA

Ice shelf

Description: A massive slab of ice that is attached to the land but which floats on the sea.

How it forms: From an ice sheet or glacier that flows out to sea. The shelf stays fixed to the ice sheet and icebergs break off the end and float away. Ice shelves can be enormous. The Ross Ice Shelf in Antarctica is about the same size as the whole of France.

Sea ice

Description: A Thin layer of ice over the sea.

How it forms: From frozen seawater. The Arctic Ocean and some of the Southern Ocean freezes solid in winter. In fact, winter sea ice almost doubles the size of Antarctica. It's only a few metres thick and mostly melts away in summer. Pack ice consists of broken bits of sea ice that drift on the wind and ocean currents. The sort of sea ice that clings to the coast is called fast ice. All horribly hazardous to ships.

But these four cool customers are just the tip of the iceberg. You'll have to visit Gloria's Uncle Gino's polar ice-cream parlour to check out the rest. Go on, you deserve a treat. Choose from six sensationally frosty flavours. They're guaranteed to melt in your mouth.

Uncle Gino's ICE CREAM
You'd go to the ends of the Earth for it!

① FABULOUS FRAZIL ICE
A slushy mixture of needle-shaped ice crystals which float in the water.
Great for slurping through your teeth.

② PERFECT PANCAKE ICE
Round and flat like pancakes only much crunchier. These pancakes float on the sea. Grab one as the sea starts to freeze over for winter. For wide-mouthed customers only.

③ GOURMET GREASE ICE
A soupy mush of sea ice which gives the surface of water an oily sheen. For slippery customers.

④ SUNCUP SPECIAL
A gigantic ice sculpture carved from snow by the waves and wind. Looks like an enormous mushroom. Our vegetarian offering.

⑤ SASTRUGI WHIP
Ice that's been whipped into peaks and troughs by the wind. A bit like the yummy topping on a lemon meringue pie.
Hold on to your hats!

⑥ ICEBERG EXTRAVAGANZA
Today's special, this is an ice lolly like you've never had before. One of these beauties will keep you quiet for years and years.
WARNING: SEE FACT SHEET BEFORE YOU START LICKING!

Eight freezing iceberg facts

1 Icebergs are colossal chunks of ice that break away from glaciers and ice shelves. And we're not talking one or two here but thousands every year. Oddly, horrible geographers call this breaking off "calving". So you'd think a baby iceberg would be called a calf wouldn't you. But, for some reason, it isn't. Glaciologists call baby icebergs growlers. But don't worry, their bark's usually worse than their bite (the glaciologists', I mean).

2 Growlers are about the size of grand pianos which is titchy in iceberg terms. The next bergs up are called bergy bits (yes, really!). They are the size of houses, but even that's pretty paltry. Some awesome icebergs are real monsters. In Antarctica, they're like enormous ice islands and can measure a staggering 150 kilometres long and 150 metres tall. This is how awe-struck Arctic explorer, Admiral Richard E. Byrd, described his first sight of icebergs:

Stricken fleets of ice bigger by far than all the navies in the world, wandering hopelessly through a smoking gloom.

3 Incredible icebergs come in all sorts of shapes and sizes. Here's a quick spotter's guide to the main sorts. Can you spot the odd one out?

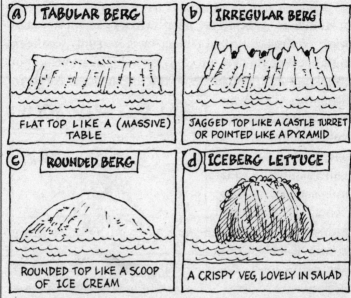

(a) TABULAR BERG
FLAT TOP LIKE A (MASSIVE) TABLE

(b) IRREGULAR BERG
JAGGED TOP LIKE A CASTLE TURRET OR POINTED LIKE A PYRAMID

(c) ROUNDED BERG
ROUNDED TOP LIKE A SCOOP OF ICE CREAM

(d) ICEBERG LETTUCE
A CRISPY VEG, LOVELY IN SALAD

4 The biggest iceberg ever was spotted off the coast of Antarctica by the crew of the USS *Glacier*. In 1956, they had the fright of their lives when a monster berg THE SIZE OF BELGIUM went floating by. Imagine an ice lolly that big! Luckily, they lived to tell the tale.

5 Which is more than can be said for the passengers and crew of the supposedly unsinkable RMS *Titanic*, the most luxurious ocean liner ever built. In April 1912, the *Titanic* was on her maiden voyage from Southampton to New York, sailing across the North Atlantic with more than 2,000 people on board. It was late at night and the sea was icy. By the time the lookouts spotted the iceberg dead ahead, it was too late to get out of the way. The lethal berg gashed a huge hole in the ship's side and water began pouring in. A few hours later, the *Titanic* sank with the tragic loss of 1,490 lives.

6 Trouble is, icebergs are horribly tricky to spot because seven-tenths of the ice lies underwater. You only see the tip of the iceberg. So they can easily rip a ship apart before you even know it. Today, planes of the International Ice Patrol scan the icy Arctic seas, warning ships of iceberg danger. And scientists also track icebergs with radar and satellites. Some icebergs are even fitted with radio transmitters to tell scientists exactly where they are.

7 Keeping tabs on an iceberg sounds simple enough. But icebergs don't hang around for very long. Big bergs can drift for thousands of kilometres on the wind and ocean currents. And they're always giving scientists the slip. Icebergs from the Arctic have been seen as far south as balmy Bermuda. Most icebergs last for about two years before they break up and melt. But some can stay frozen solid for up to 20 years...

8 Which could be horribly useful for humans. If you melted a medium-sized berg, you'd have enough water to supply a big city for weeks. Great news for dry places like Australia and the Middle East which get very little rain. There's just one teeny snag. How on Earth do you lug the iceberg all that way in one piece? Scientists think huge supertugs could be built to tow the icebergs from Antarctica. This would take about a year. Are the scientists serious? Would their crackpot scheme really work? It's probably much too costly to put into practice, but you'll have to wait and see. For the time being, their plans are on ice.

Earth-shattering fact
In Japan and Arctic Canada, companies are now selling chunks of glacier ice for cooling down trendy drinks. When the ice melts, it gives off bubbles of air which have been trapped in the ice for thousands of years. How cool is that?

Teacher teaser

Next time your teacher asks you an awkward question, ask him this one back. Smile as if a glacier ice cube wouldn't melt in your mouth, and put up your hand and say:

He'll be so gobsmacked, he'll forget what he asked you. But what on Earth are you talking about?

Answer: Incredibly, the answer is yes, it can! To find out more about ice, glaciologists drill deep holes and pull out long sticks of ice, like giant ice lollies, which they call ice cores. By counting the layers in the ice, they can tell how old the ice

is. Scientists recently drilled an ice core 3 kilometres long in Antarctica. They reckon the ancient ice at the bottom is a staggering 250,000 years old. Core blimey!

HELP! IT'S A NUNATAK!

No, no, no. It's nothing to do with nuns. A nunatak is (noon-attack) a polar peak or island that pokes out above the ice sheet. Actually, it comes from a local Inuit word for attached land.

For intrepid British explorer, Sir Ernest Shackleton (1874–1922), nunataks were the least of his worries. If he never saw ice again in his life, it wouldn't be a day too soon. Now that your teeth have stopped chattering, check out this amazing true tale…

Icebound in Antarctica, 1914–1917

As a lad, Sir Ernest Shackleton dreamed of seeing the world. You could say adventure was in his blood. He was only 16 when he left school and ran away to sea. Later, he went to nautical college and became a master sailor. He almost reached the South Pole twice (once with Captain Scott)

SHACKLETON

but had been beaten back by woeful weather. Now he wanted to be the first person to cross the icy Antarctic continent. But first he needed a crew. The story goes that he put an advert in the paper:

> Men wanted for hazardous journey,
> Small wages, bitter cold.
> Long months of complete darkness,
> Constant danger, safe return doubtful.
> Honour and recognition in case of success.

Would you have signed up? No way? Luckily for Ernest, applications flooded in. And from 5,000 hopeful volunteers, he picked the pluckiest. On 1 August 1914, he and his crew of 28 men set sail from England on board their sturdy ship, the *Endurance*. Ahead of them lay a desperate journey across the most hostile habitat on Earth. A journey no one had ever tried before. Their last port of call before Antarctica was the tiny island of South Georgia. Then it was south into the unknown.

In December, the *Endurance* sailed into the treacherous, ice-infested waters of the Weddell Sea. Battling through the perilous pack ice was no picnic. For weeks, they tried to find a clear channel through the constantly drifting ice floes. But their efforts were in vain. Then, on 19 January 1915, disaster struck. The *Endurance* stuck fast in the pack ice, just one day's sail from their destination at Vahsel Bay. Soon she was frozen solid, "like an almond in a piece of toffee", one man wrote.

As the pack ice dragged *Endurance* ever further away from land, Shackleton knew his dream was over. Summer was nearly gone – it would be impossible to cross the continent now, even if they could reach it. They would have to spend winter on the ice.

At first, the ship was safe enough for the men to live on board. But for how long? Nobody knew. One of two things might happen. Come spring, the ice might thaw and free the ship. Or the shifting ice floes could crush it to pieces, like a fragile eggshell. (An ice floe's a chunk of floating sea ice.) By October, the signs were ominous. With a rumbling sound like thunder, the floes tightened their icy grip. Before the crew's disbelieving eyes, the *Endurance* began to break up.

Her timbers groaned and cracked under the pressure, and she sprung leak after leak. As she listed to one side, Shackleton gave orders to abandon ship. The men salvaged what they could, including the three lifeboats, and pitched camp on the ice. Their only hope was that the ice would carry them within reach of land. Otherwise, the future looked horribly bleak. With no radio contact, no one knew where on Earth they where.

Some weeks later, on 21 November, Shackleton and his men watched sadly as the *Endurance* sank beneath the ice.

Nightmare at sea

For months, the men drifted on the ice. But by April, it was obvious the ice was splitting up, right beneath their feet. At any minute it could give way – their camp was no longer safe. Shackleton ordered the lifeboats to be launched – they would try to make for land, however desperate the journey was. And desperate it was. They braved icebergs and gale-force winds that could tear a boat to pieces. The men took it in turns at rowing. But by the end of the watch, their hands were so icy cold they had to be chipped from the oars. At night, they camped on the ice floe, until it became too dangerous. One night, a gigantic crack suddenly opened up and a man plunged into the perishing sea in his sleeping-bag. Shackleton managed to haul him out but they'd learned their lesson. After that they slept in the lifeboats. At last, after an appalling six-day journey, they reached a rocky island called Elephant Island on the Northern Antarctic Peninsula and stumbled on to the stony, ice-covered beach. It was the first time the men had set foot on solid land for 497 days.

But their celebrations didn't last long. On this isolated island, there was no hope of rescue. No one ever came near this awful place. What's more, another wretched winter was looming... Shackleton knew there was only one thing for it. He would have to go for help. Taking five men with him, Shackleton set out in one of the lifeboats. It was a horribly risky thing to do. He decided to head back to South Georgia and its whaling station, some 1,200 kilometres away ... across the stormiest seas in the world. For days, the men fought to keep their little boat afloat as it was tossed by giant waves and tearing winds. It was so cold the sea spray froze on the boat, caking it in thick ice. Despite the constant pitching and rolling, the men had to risk their lives chipping it off. Otherwise the boat would have sunk.

The only shelter from the weather was a canvas cover stretched over the bow. But conditions inside were hellish.

There was only enough space for three men to go in at a time. And it was wet, cramped and bitterly cold. Like being buried alive.

Frostbitten, exhausted and sodden, and with just two days' water left, it seemed they couldn't last long. Then, after 17 desperate days at sea, a piece of seaweed floated by – a sure sign of land!

But they weren't safe yet. With South Georgia in their sights, the weather suddenly changed for the worse. Hurricane-force winds drove them towards the sheer cliffs, threatening to smash the boat to pieces. It took a superhuman effort, but somehow they managed to steer into a cove.

The last leg
There was just one small snag – the whaling station lay on the far side of the island. And it was too risky to sail round. There was only one answer: some of them would have to set out on foot. It was a terrible setback for the exhausted men who were already on their last legs. As the crow flies, the whaling station was only 35 kilometres away. But it might as well have been on the moon. No one had ever attempted to cross the island before – and there were no useful maps. Between them and the station lay perilous peaks, capped

with glaciers and pitted with killer crevasses. But it was a risk they had to take. On 19 May, Shackleton set out with two men, a rope, an ice-axe and three days' supplies stuffed into their socks. For extra grip, they banged nails from the boat into the soles of their boots. Then, for 36 exhausting

hours, the three men slogged on, hardly daring to stop and rest. One false step and they'd plummet into the icy sea and certain death.

At last, on the afternoon of 20 May, they stumbled into the whaling station. Against all the odds, they'd made it. Filthy and wild-looking, Shackleton approached the startled manager.

"My name is Shackleton," he said.

It turned out they'd reached safety just in time. That night, a biting blizzard blew up that would have killed them if they'd been caught in it. Later that year, Shackleton sailed for Elephant Island to rescue his stranded men. Incredibly, despite their appalling ordeal, not a single life had been lost.

Test your teacher

Ernest Shackleton would have made a brilliant teacher. He was intelligent, brave, cheerful and a born leader. What a hero! What d'ya mean, that doesn't sound like any teacher you know? He was also one of the most famous explorers ever. So famous that even your own geography teacher will know all about him. In fact, it's probably his specialist subject. Try this quick quiz to find out.

1 Shackleton's ship was called *Endurance*. Why?

a) It was an old family motto.

b) It came from the back of a cereal packet.

c) It was the name of a famous sea battle.

2 On the way to Antarctica, the ship's cat, Mrs Chippy, fell overboard. What did Shackleton do?

a) Left it to perish.

b) Turned round and went back for it.

c) Threw it some ship's mice to eat.

3 What was Shackleton's nickname?

a) Bossy Boots.

b) Grumpy Drawers.

c) The Boss.

4 What did Shackleton's parents want him to be?

a) A doctor.

b) An explorer.

c) A vet.

5 Which of these books did Shackleton write?

a) *Perishing Poles.*

b) *South.*

c) *The Heart of the Antarctic.*

One thing's for certain. Getting to grips with awesome ice is a risky thing to do. If your ship isn't smashed to smithereens, you might end up in the freezing drink. Count yourself lucky. You can always nip off home and have a nice, hot drink while you thaw out your frostbitten feet. The hardy creatures you're about to meet are well and truly left out in the cold.

Some people think they're real tough nuts. You know the sort I mean. In winter, while you're wrapped up like an Egyptian mummy, they're wearing a vest and telling everyone how brilliantly hot it is.

But are they really as hardy as they seem? What if the temperature was a f-f-freezing -20°C? And what if it was accompanied by pitch darkness, and spine-chilling winds? Perfect polar conditions, in fact. Surely nothing could live at the ends of the Earth without freezing to death?

Incredibly, for hundreds of horribly hardy plants and animals, the perishing Poles are home, sweet home. How on Earth do they survive in their hostile habitat? Why not drop in at the world's first (and only) perishing polar pet shop...

HORRIBLE HEALTH WARNING

Some of these pets can be horribly dangerous. Especially if they're hungry. So if you're thinking of training them to fetch your slippers or use the remote-control, DON'T BOTHER! By the way, your new polar pet will need a nice, cold place to live, preferably outdoors. If you keep it in the house, turn off the central heating. If it gets too hot, it'll die.

Perishing polar pet shop

Are you a lonely geographer? Are you looking for a little friend, someone to snuggle up to on those nippy polar nights?

Look no further! For your perfect pet, visit our Polar Pet Shop. We guarantee you won't find any fluffy bunnies or gormless goldfish here...

The Ice fish has got antifreeze in its blood, like the stuff your dad puts in the car in winter. This stops the freaky fish from freezing to death. Now is that cool, or what? And don't worry if you forget to feed your fish. It's used to going hungry. In the icy ocean, food's sometimes hard to find. No wonder this unfussy fish will guzzle anything, given half a chance.

① ENT-ICE-ING ICE FISH:
DESCRIPTION: A SEE-THROUGH FISH WITH GREAT BIG TEETH, A BIG SNOUT AND BIG EYES. A BIT LIKE A FISHY GHOST.
SIZE: YOU'LL NEED A WHOPPING TANK FOR THIS PET - IT CAN GROW 60 CENTIMETRES LONG.
HABITAT: SOUTHERN OCEAN.

The Arctic fox is perfectly colour co-ordinated. In summer, it grows a thin, brown-grey coat to match the tundra* rocks. It's the perfect disguise for sneaking up on its prey. In winter, it changes into a thick, white coat to blend in with the ice and keep it warm.

In summer, small furry creatures called lemmings are this cunning creature's favourite snack. In winter, the fox follows polar bears and scoffs their left-overs.

POLAR CHUNKS

POLA CHUN

POL CHU

PENGUIN PELLETS

PENGUIN PELLETS

PENGUIN PELLETS

② FABULOUS ARCTIC FOX.
DESCRIPTION: ER, LIKE A FOX ACTUALLY. (WELL WHAT DID YOU EXPECT?)
HABITAT: ARCTIC SEA ICE AND TUNDRA.

* The tundra's a vast stretch of icy wasteland around the North Pole. It's covered in short, scrubby plants but it's too cold for trees to grow. In winter, the top of the tundra's frozen but it thaws out in summer.

Despite their lousy appearance, isopods make fascinating pets. For a start, they grow, and move, very slowly (thank goodness for that!). That's because the water's so icy cold, they need to save energy and there's not much food about.

It feeds on seabed scraps, including worms, sea-bed creatures and lumps of nourishing seal poo.

③ ENORMOUS ISOPOD:
DESCRIPTION: LIKE A GIANT, AND WE MEAN **GIANT** WOODLOUSE.
SIZE: 17 CENTIMETRES LONG (AS LONG AS TEN ORDINARY WOODLICE).
HABITAT: SOUTHERN OCEAN SEABED.

I'D HATE TO FIND ONE OF **THEM** IN MY PYJAMAS!

You might have trouble keeping track of the globe-trotting Arctic tern – it loves travelling. It escapes the northern winter blues by spending summer in Antarctica. Then it heads back to the Arctic for summer again. That way, good weather is guaranteed and it picks up a fish supper or two on the way. Fancy packing your bags and tagging along? It's a round trip of 40,000 kilometres.

④ GLOBE-TROTTING ARCTIC TERN:
DESCRIPTION: WHITE BIRD WITH A BLACK HEAD, BRIGHT RED BEAK AND LONG FORKED TAIL. SMALL, BUT CUTS A DASH. HABITAT: ARCTIC AND ANTARCTICA.

⑤ SLINKY WEDDELL SEAL: DESCRIPTION: LARGE AND LUMBERING WITH A SMALL HEAD AND BIG EYES. SLEEK GREY COAT WITH BLACK AND GREY SPOTS. SIZE: 3 METRES LONG AND WEIGHS UP TO HALF A TONNE. HABITAT: THE SEA ICE AROUND ANTARCTICA.

The Weddell seal mostly lives under the ice where it's warmer. It uses its teeth to gnaw breathing holes in the ice. (No wonder they're always falling out.) A thick layer of blubber (fat) under its skin keeps it warm.

It feeds on deep-sea fish and squid. Luckily, seals are brilliant deep-sea divers and can hold their breath for an hour while they're hunting for food. (DON'T try this at home, however peckish you feel.)

The Polar Pet Shop presents
☆ CREATURE OF THE WEEK ☆

THE POLAR PET SHOP IS PROUD TO PRESENT THIS WEEK'S CREATURE OF THE WEEK...THE COOLEST POLAR PET AROUND...THE PERISHING

☆ POLAR BEAR ☆

DESCRIPTION: HUGE WHITE BEAR!

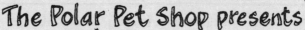

SHARP TEETH: FOR GRABBING AND CHEWING PREY (WATCH OUT YOU'RE NOT ON THE MENU)

SMALL HEAD AND EARS: FOR CUTTING DOWN HEAT LOSS

LONG NOSE: FOR HEATING THE FREEZING AIR BEFORE IT REACHES THE BEAR'S LUNGS AND FOR SNIFFING OUT SEALS

WHITE FUR: FOR CAMOUFLAGE ON THE ICE

FURRY PAWS: LIKE SNOW-SHOES FOR WALKING OVER SOFT SNOW WITHOUT SINKING THEY'RE ALSO PADDLE-SHAPED FOR SWIMMING

SHARP CLAWS: FOR KEEPING A GRIP ON THE SLIPPERY ICE AND SWIPING AT SEALS

THICK FUR COAT: FOR KEEPING OUT THE COLD. THE HAIRS ARE HOLLOW FOR TRAPPING THE SUN'S HEAT, AND OILY TO KEEP THE BEAR WATERPROOF. UNDERNEATH, THERE'S A THICK LAYER OF BLUBBER (FAT) FOR WARMTH. HANDILY, THIS CAN ALSO BE CONVERTED INTO FOOD AND WATER

If you're thinking of getting a polar bear as a pet, here's a word of warning. Looking after a polar bear isn't easy. Forget saucers of milk or little fishy treats. Polar bears are no pussy-cats. Still keen? OK, here are some handy hints and tips on polar-bear care.

POLAR BEAR PET-OWNER'S MANUAL

• Get a really BIG bed for your new pet. In fact, get a really big house – polar bears are massive. I've come across bears on my travels that weigh a tonne and stand a towering three metres tall (that's about twice as tall as you). Imagine taking that for a walk! They're the biggest, most powerful carnivores (meat-eaters) around so my advice to you is: keep clear of those seriously sharp teeth.

• Take your bear to the swimming pool. Your polar bear will need plenty of exercise. But forget walkies. Polar bears are superb swimmers (they do a sort of doggy paddle). And they can keep it up for days. Don't worry if your bear goes missing. When they fancy a rest, they hop on an ice floe and drift off, sometimes for hundreds of kilometres.

KEEP UP!

• Stock up on seal steaks. Ordinary pet food won't do. Polar bears love juicy seal steaks or better still, juicy whole seals. Polar bears are sneaky hunters. They wait by a seal's breathing hole, covering their black noses with their paws for extra camouflage. Then, when a seal pops up for air, the bear bashes it on the head. Nice! A sharp-nosed bear can sniff a seal out over a kilometre away, even if it's lurking beneath the ice.

SNIFF! SNIFF!

• House-train your polar bear. If you dare. They've got some horrible habits, I can tell you. When there isn't much food about, they come into town and rummage about in people's dustbins. In Churchill, Canada, pilfering polar bears are such pests, they're rounded up and put in a polar bear jail! Frequent offenders are given a sedative to make them sleepy and carried away by helicopter. They're taken off somewhere safe, a long way from the town.

- Don't be fooled by their cute appearance. Polar bear cubs look sweet, don't they? Especially on Christmas cards. But looks can be deceptive. They might be all wide-eyed and fluffy now but, like puppies and kittens, they soon grow up. And they start learning to hunt almost as soon as they can walk. So if you're going to try cuddling a polar bear cub, expect a nasty nip or two. Ouch!

Earth-shattering fact

There aren't any polar bears in Antarctica. In fact, there aren't any big land animals at all. It's too parky for them to live. The largest year-round resident is a minute flightless midge. This titchy insect's just 12 millimetres long – that's this big:

In case you were wondering, there's no point in the midge having wings because it's too bloomin' windy to fly. Even teenier mites (they're close relations of spiders) live up seals' nostrils. Great if they could be trained to pick their noses too.

P-p-p-pick up a penguin

If you don't have room for a polar bear, and mites are a mite irritating, why not p-p-p-pick up a penguin instead. Now you might think a penguin's a silly-looking bird that looks as if it's dressed up like a waiter in a posh restaurant. And of course, you'd be right. But when it comes to staying alive in the bitter cold, plucky penguins are no bird brains. Take the emperor penguin, for example.

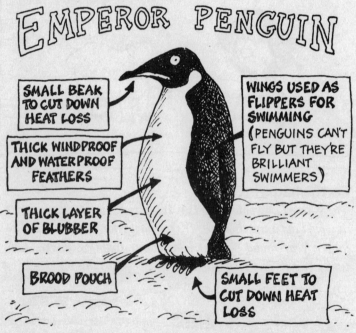

EMPEROR PENGUIN

SMALL BEAK TO CUT DOWN HEAT LOSS

THICK WINDPROOF AND WATERPROOF FEATHERS

THICK LAYER OF BLUBBER

BROOD POUCH

WINGS USED AS FLIPPERS FOR SWIMMING (PENGUINS CAN'T FLY BUT THEY'RE BRILLIANT SWIMMERS)

SMALL FEET TO CUT DOWN HEAT LOSS

A cold snap doesn't rattle an emperor penguin. They're much too tough for that. In fact, they find the freezing temperatures so bracing they spend the winter on the Antarctic ice when the weather's at its worst. Their babies are even born there. Imagine you were an emperor penguin chick. Would you be able to survive?

Could you be an emperor penguin?

1 You start off life as a large egg about 12 centimetres long which your mum lays on to her feet. Then she scarpers. She heads off to sea to hunt for fish while your dad's left holding the baby.

2 Your dad balances the egg on top of his feet and covers it with a furry flap of skin. The flap's called a brood pouch, and it keeps the egg warm and snug. If it falls on to the freezing ice, the chick inside will die.

3 And there your dad stays for 60 days and 60 nights without food or shelter. Even though the temperature may drop to -40°C and he's battered by blizzards. Brave, isn't he? But your dad's not the only one. He joins thousands of other males who huddle together for warmth.

4 You hatch out in the middle of winter. Brrr! Your dad carries you about on his feet until you're about eight weeks old. Then you grow a thick, fluffy feather coat to keep you warm.

5 Your doting dad hasn't eaten for months and he's horribly skinny and thin. Luckily, your mum comes back. Just in the nick of time. Your ravenous dad waddles off to sea for a well-earned feast, while your mum sicks up some fish for your supper. Lovely.

6 By mid-summer, you're old enough to look after yourself. You leave home and head out to sea for some fishing. But watch out for leopard seals lurking at the edge of the ice. Their favourite meal is, guess what? Yep, young penguins.

Life in the polar seas

You need to be seriously tough to survive on land, but it's a different story in the polar seas. Even though the water's bitterly cold, it's teeming with life. That's because there's plenty of food for peckish polar creatures to guzzle. The animals in the sea are joined in a food chain. That's the name horrible scientists use to describe the links between animals and the creatures they gobble. Most food chains start off with plants. A typical food chain goes something like this:

A food chain in the perishing Southern Ocean goes something like this:

The secret diary of a krill

Krill are little pink shrimp-like creatures a paltry five centimetres long. Real small fry. So you might think it would take an awesome amount of krill to fill a blue whale up. And you'd be right. Blue whales have truly enormous appetites. They can eat a staggering FOUR TONNES of krill … EVERY DAY. Imagine eating that much school dinner! And they're not the only ones. Greedy sea birds, penguins, seals and fish also gorge themselves silly on krill. So you see krill are vitally important in the polar food chain. But what's it like for the krill? I mean, it can't be much fun being chased around all day, then gobbled up for lunch. What if a krill could keep a secret diary? (OK, so you're really going to have to stretch your imagination for this bit…)

69

The Southern Ocean, Midsummer

1 p.m. Spent lunchtime swimming around with mates, minding own business. Felt a bit peckish so stopped off for a scrumptious snack of ice algae.

1.10 p.m. Huh! Just about to grab a snack when a blue whale blundered by. Bloomin' big mouth. Why can't they pick on someone their own size? And talk about terrible table manners. They swim along with mouths wide open (don't they know it's rude?).

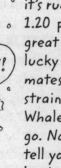

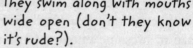

1.20 p.m. Got swept up in its great gob, the big bully. Made lucky escape with some of me mates, but unlucky ones got strained out of the water. Whale lunch. What a way to go. No fun being a krill, I can tell you. You need eyes in the back of your head.

Later that day...

3 p.m. Aaaagghh! Here we go again. It's coming to get me. And its big, fat mouth is watering. I want my mummy!

A few minutes later...

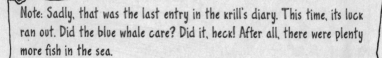

Note: Sadly, that was the last entry in the krill's diary. This time, its luck ran out. Did the blue whale care? Did it, heck! After all, there were plenty more fish in the sea.

Krill swim about in massive swarms, weighing up to ten million tonnes each. These swarms are so huge they can be spotted by ships' radar and even by satellites in outer space. Scientists reckon there are about 600 million million krill in the Southern Ocean (that's 100 times as many people on Earth). Which makes them pretty tough for blue whales to miss.

HORRIBLE HEALTH WARNING

Fancy tucking into a nice plate of sausage and chips? Krill sausage and chips, that is. And what about krill and cream cheese sandwiches? Believe it or not, krill cuisine is catching on fast with horrible humans. Trouble is, you'd need to scoff it down fast – krill goes off very quickly. Phwoar!

Plucky polar plants

Most plants love warm, sunny weather with the odd light shower of rain. They're perfect conditions for plants to bloom. Conditions you'd never get at the perishing poles. You might think that faced with the cold, dry and windy conditions polar plants would curl up and die. But surprisingly, some plants manage to grow in them. Here's the low-down for all those plants out there who might be thinking of emigrating:

1 Don't bother with soil. Some Antarctic algae (tiny single-celled plants) have got little hairs for swimming in the snow. That way they can reach the sunlight which they need for making food. And to stop their bodies freezing, they make a kind of antifreeze. In some places, algae turn the snow bright pink, like raspberry ripple ice cream. The plants' red colouring works a bit like suncream and stops them getting sunburnt in the super-strong polar sun. Ingenious, eh?

2 Don't be fussy about what you eat. Lichen are ideal plants for the poles because they'll even feed on bare rock. The lichens make acids which dissolve the rock and make it crumble. Then they send out tiny "roots" to suck up nourishing goodness from the rock. They use this to make food. Other lichens live on seal or penguin poo left on the rock. Lovely!

3 Learn to live anywhere. Some Antarctic algae actually live inside solid rock. These picky plants prefer dark-coloured rocks which soak up the sun's heat (it's the albedo effect again). They're also out of the biting wind. The algae creep into the rock through minute cracks. They're kept alive by sunlight filtering through the see-through grains in the rock.

4 Grow as slowly as possible. That's how lichens survive the bitter cold. At the perishing poles, there may only be one day every year when it's warm enough to grow. So a patch of lichen the size of a cabbage leaf may be hundreds of years old. Even soggy school dinner cabbage isn't that old!

5 Forget flowering in winter. It's too bloomin' dark and cold. But when spring comes, polar flowers burst into bloom. Mind you, they have to be quick and spread their seeds before the next cold snap bites.

6 Keep your head down. Polar trees aren't tall and bushy like the trees you see outside. In fact, they're so small you could step right over the top. Trees, like Arctic willows, grow very low and spindly to keep out of the howling wind. Like long-lived lichens, they grow in slow motion. A willow stem as thick as a pencil may be hundreds of years old. (By the way, there aren't any trees in Antarctica at all.)

But bird-brained penguins, whopping whales and pint-sized polar trees aren't the only weird wildlife you'll find at the poles. Some humans find the freezing conditions rather refreshing, in fact. Are they stark, raving mad or just very well wrapped up? Why not nip along into the next chapter and meet up with a few of them?

GOING MY WAY?

PERISHING POLAR PEOPLE

Polar living may be cool for polar bears. But what about human beings? Astonishingly, some hardy humans actually choose to live near the North Pole, despite the horribly hostile conditions. So how on Earth do these polar people cope with their icy lifestyle? Who better to ask than the local Inuit people of the Arctic. They've lived on the ice all their lives.

By the way, no one lives permanently at the parky South Pole – it's just too teeth-chatteringly cold. But you might bump into the odd batty Antarctic scientist or two a bit later on in this chapter.

Polar people

The Inuit (Ee-noo-eet) mainly live in icy Alaska, northern Canada and Greenland. In the Inuit language, their name means "the people". Traditionally, the Inuit roamed the Arctic, fishing and hunting animals for food. Their lives were ruled by the changing seasons. In summer, they hunted seals, whales and walruses near the coast, and stocked up with food for winter. In winter, they moved inland to hunt caribou (reindeer). The Inuit relied on the land and sea for everything they used, and treated their icy home with great respect, taking care not to do any harm.

So how on Earth do the Inuit do it? Are you ready to find out how they survive? If you're planning on paying the Inuit a visit, be warned. You might think you've got it tough with too much homework and too little pocket money. But at least you don't risk freezing to death every time you nip out of your front door. Living in the Arctic is horribly hard. The Inuit know the ice like the back of their hands, and they're experts at polar survival. Even so, one false move and they, and you, could easily be a goner.

If you want to learn to live like a local, why not sneak a look in our essential Inuit Polar survival guide. It's packed full of life-saving hints and tips. Just ask good old Gloria – she wouldn't leave home without it.

Teacher teaser

Is your teacher always showing off about how many languages she can speak? Boring, isn't it? Try this tongue-twisting teaser to get your own back. When your teacher asks for your homework, smile sweetly and say:

PLEASE, MISS. I HAVEN'T FINISHED IT. YOU SEE, MY QARASAASIAQ'S ON THE BLINK

Do you need to see the doctor?

Answer: No, there's nothing wrong with you. Qarasaasiaq's the word for computer in the Inuktitut language (that's the lingo spoken by the Inuit). It's made up of three words which mean "little artificial brain". If the Inuit don't have word for something, they simply make one up. Do you take sugar in your tea? Then you'll need to ask for some siorasat "looks like sand". Clever, eh?

Perishing Polar Survival for Beginners by the Inuit

Lesson 1. What to wear

If you're heading off to the perishing Poles, you need to dress for the part. But forget looking cool. It's keeping warm that counts. And chucking on an extra jumper won't do, I'm afraid. (Even if your dear old granny knitted it for Christmas.) You need to wear layers of clothes that'll trap warm air next to your skin, and let sweat escape (otherwise it'll draw the warmth away and could freeze on your skin). To stay really warm and snug, take a look at what the locals are wearing. Then model your clothes on theirs. Here's the best in Inuit cool.

This is a traditional Inuit costume which was worn for hundreds of years. Today, many of the Inuit buy modern clothes from a company called the Hudson's Bay Company or by mail-order instead.

NICE!

Earth-shattering fact

An anorak isn't a really naff mac worn by nerds, whatever you might think. In the Inuit language, an annuraaq's *the word for a really cool coat – well, a really warm one actually.*

CARIBOU SKIN COAT: Worn fur side out. Animal skin is brilliantly warm and windproof. Wear a thinner sealskin or bird skin tunic underneath with the furry side turned towards your skin.

FOX OR WOLF FUR TRIM AROUND HOOD: Stops your breath freezing on your skin.

POLAR BEAR SKIN TROUSERS: Worn fur side out. Tuck into your boots to keep out draughts. Wear a thinner pair of sealskin or fox fur trousers underneath, fur side in.

SEALSKIN MITTENS: You can also pull your hands inside your sleeves to stop your fingers getting frostbite.

MUKLUKS: (Sealskin boots) With a pair of sheepskin or sealskin socks worn underneath, fur side facing in. If it's very cold, wear several pairs of boots, one on top of the other.

Bootiful boots

If you fancy a new pair of trainers, you can just pop along to a shoeshop. Easy-peasy. But in the icy Arctic, there aren't many shops around. So the horribly handy Inuit traditionally make all their own clothes. Got a strong stomach? You'll need one for the next bit. You're about to find out how the Inuit make their mukluks (sealskin boots).

Note:

In the past, millions of seals were killed for their fur coats by large-scale seal hunters. But this is now strictly controlled. The Inuit are granted special seal-hunting rights because they need seal meat and fur to survive, and don't simply kill seals for sport or luxury.

1 First the Inuit catch a seal. It's trickier than it looks. Seals spend most of their time in the water, under the ice. Luckily, the Inuit are experts. They know exactly where to find a secretive seal's breathing hole. How? Well, they look for signs of teeth marks in the ice, or they sniff out the seal's strong pong.

2 They wait by the breathing hole, their harpoon ready in their hands. (Today, most Inuit use rifles instead. Unfortunately, they sometimes miss and the loud bang scares the seals away.) They need to be patient. Very patient. It might be hours before the seal comes up for air.

3 Once the seal has been harpooned, it's skinned and the meat is cut into chunks. The Inuit love eating seal, cooked or raw. Dried seal intestines are a particular delicacy. In fact, the only bit of a seal you can't eat is the greasy gall bladder. Any leftovers are deep frozen for winter.

4 The sealskin's stretched out and the blubber's scraped off with a knife. (They don't throw the blubber away – it makes brilliant fuel for lamps and cooking stoves.) Inuit boot-makers take care not to nick the skin, then they soak it in wee, yes, wee, overnight to get it nice and clean. The next step is to rinse it and peg it out to dry.

5 Only now can they start on their boots. They measure their feet and legs with pieces of string. Then they cut out two soles and two uppers from the sealskin. The sealskin's too tough to sew, so they chew it to make it softer. Then they sew the boots together. Traditionally, the Inuit used seal bone needles and seal sinew thread. (Today, people often use dental floss as thread instead!)

6 They turn the tops over and thread through a drawstring. Now their boots are ready to wear.

Seal souls

One thing the Inuit never forget to do is thank Sedna, the sea goddess, for the seals they catch. They believe that animals have a soul, just like human beings. If you don't show the seal respect, Sedna blows her top. Not a pretty sight. When Sedna's mad, the story goes, her hair gets dirty and matted, and the seals get tangled in it, so there aren't any left to hunt. If this happens, one of the Inuit goes into a deep, deep trance. In his mind's eye, he visits stroppy Sedna's undersea den and combs her hair to set the seals free. Talk about having a bad hair day.

I'M OFF TO SORT OUT SEDNA

Lesson 2: What to eat

OK, so now you've got your polar clothes, what about something to eat? The Arctic's too bloomin' cold to grow fruit and veg, so the Inuit mainly eat fish, fat and meat. And you thought school dinners were boring! Actually, their odd-sounding diet's disgustingly healthy and crammed full of vital vitamins, (unlike your school dinners). After a good day's hunting, the Inuit have a fabulous feast to share out the food they've caught. And guess what? Yep, you're invited.

INUIT FEAST MENU ∽

Starters
• *A selection of delicious dips*
Served with slices of freeze-dried seal or caribou meat.

Dip 1 Tender morsels of lean caribou or seal, mixed with blood and melted fat. Seasoned with ptarmigan (a type of bird) intestine.

Dip 2 Chunks of seal or whale blubber stored in a cool place until it rots and turns into liquid.

Dip 3 The half-digested contents of a caribou's stomach. Pick out any clumps of grass and leaves.

Main course

- Kiviak (kee-vee-yak).

A type of sausage, with a tasty twist. It's a delicacy in Greenland, especially at weddings. Here's the recipe, if you fancy making it at home:

What you need:

- about 300 little auks (tiny seabirds)
- a sealskin, still lined with blubber

What you do:

1 Stuff the sealskin with the little auks, then sew it up.

2 Bury it under a pile of rocks and leave it to rot.

3 Wait for six months, then dig it up again.

4 If it stinks like smelly cheese, it's ready to eat!

Note: Eat the kiviak with your fingers, taking care to pick out any feathers, bones and beaks that might get stuck in your teeth.

Optional side dishes

- *Narwhal (a type of whale) skin strips*
Chewy, with a nice, nutty taste.
- *Mashed seal brain*
Served warm.
- *Succulent lichen*
Cut from a caribou's stomach.

Pudding
- *Caribou surprise*
Forget spotted dick and custard. This pungent pudding is made from blood warmed in a freshly-killed caribou's stomach. Bet that's a surpise to you!

Horrible Health Warning
If you fancy liver and onions, make sure the liver isn't from a polar bear. It contains massive amounts of Vitamin A which can be lethal for human beings.

Lesson 3: Finding shelter

Today, many Inuit live in small, wooden houses in modern towns. Traditionally, they lived in sealskin tents in summer and, in winter, in stone and earth homes built underground. But what if you're out on a hunting trip and a blizzard starts to blow? You need a warm, windproof shelter for a night or two, but there's nothing except snow for miles around. Don't panic, help is at hand. Here's how to build an igloo, or snow house, the most famous type of Inuit shelter of all.

What you need:
- a knife (made from bone or walrus ivory) or a saw
- some nice firm snow

What you do:

1 Lie down in the snow and stretch your arms and legs out. Draw a big circle around you by moving your arms and legs up and down (like making a snow "angel").

2 Cut out about 30 blocks of snow, each one about the size of a large suitcase.

3 Lay some of the blocks in a circle, then build up more blocks in a spiral to make a dome shape.

4 Fit a final block on top but leave a hole for ventilation.

5 Plug any cracks with snow.

6 Cut an entrance tunnel in one side, below the level of the floor (this stops cold air getting in).

Top tip: Snow's a brilliant material for building with because it traps heat. Inside your igloo, you'll be warm and snug, no matter how perishing cold it is outside. By the way, it takes an expert Inuit builder less than an hour to put up a perfect igloo. How long do you think it would take you?

The Inuit have lived in the Arctic for thousands of years, using their amazing survival skills. But today their lives are changing. Many Inuit have been forced to give up their ancient nomadic lifestyle and move into settlements with mod cons instead. Some of these have made the Inuit's life easier, like supermarkets, rifles and motorized snowmobiles. But some people are worried about their traditional lifestyle dying out. And that would be a terrible tragedy. But it isn't all doom and gloom: some Inuit are fighting back. In 1999, a new territory was created in northern Canada. It's called Nunavut (Noo-na-voot) which means "Our Land" and it's run by and for the Inuit.

South Pole science

Meanwhile, at the South Pole, it's a different story. You see, it's too perishing cold to live there permanently. But you could always spend your hols there (it's costly so you'll need to start saving up, see page 113 for how to get there), or you could work there as a scientist. Amazingly, thousands of long-suffering scientists and support staff work in Antarctica, despite the cold and wind. So why on Earth do they do it? Well, Antarctica's an unbelievably brilliant place for science. For a start, it's the biggest laboratory in the world. And there's nowhere else on the planet like it. But this isn't the sort of science you study at school – you know, the seriously boring sort you can't stay awake in. No, this is science like never before. It's horribly exciting. Forget dull-as-ditchwater experiments and tedious test tubes. This is all about groovy glaciers, deep-frozen fossils, weird wildlife and lots more. Cool, or what?

Could you be a perishing polar scientist?

Do you have what it takes to work at the Poles? Try this quick quiz to see if you're suitable:

1 Are you frightfully fit and healthy? Yes/No
2 Do you like going camping? Yes/No
3 Are you always hungry? Yes/No
4 Do you look good in goggles? Yes/No
5 Are you easy going? Yes/No
6 Are you good at languages? Yes/No
7 Do you hate having a bath? Yes/No

8 Are you neat and tidy? Yes/No
9 Do you have beard?
Yes/No

How did you do?

7-9 yeses: Congratulations! You've really kept your cool. You'll make a brilliant beaker (that's scientists' code for a, er, scientist).

4-6 yeses: Not bad. But perhaps you'd be better off doing something less d-ice-y instead.

3 yeses and below: Oh dear! Polar science is not for you. Try something less adventurous altogether. Something like your geography homework!

OK all you beakers out there, you've done really well and you probably think you're a dead cert for a job. But that was just first base. Check out what you're really letting yourself in for below…

1 Fit and healthy? You'll need to be -- there's a lot of hard slog involved in polar science. You'll be given a thorough medical examination before you're allowed to go. Being sporty helps. Rock climbing's especially useful for rescuing people from crevasses (huge cracks in the ice). Mind you don't fall in.

2 Fond of camping? You'd better get used to it. In Antarctica, scientists mostly live on research stations. Some are like small towns with living quarters, science labs, kitchens, hospital, library, gym and their own electricity supply. One station's even got a bowling alley. But scientists also spend months out on freezing field trips where camping's a must. A pyramid tent's best to take because its shape is great in strong winds. But don't forget to mark your camp-site with a flag. Just in case a blizzard blows in and buries it in snow.

3 Always hungry? In Antarctica you burn loads of energy simply keeping warm. Not to mention all the hard work you'll have to do. So you need plenty to eat. In fact, on field trips scientists scoff about 3,500 calories a day – that's twice what you'd normally eat. The food's mostly freeze-dried so it's light and easy to lug about. You simply mix it with water (made from melted ice) and bingo, you've got lunch. Some stations have their own greenhouses so they can grow fresh salad and veg.

4 Look good in goggles? Like it or not, you'll need to wear them to protect your eyes from the sun's glare. It's especially

strong in Antarctica because it reflects off the ice and snow. Without goggles or strong sunglasses, you could get snow-blindness and not be able to see for hours, or even days. Nasty. But goggles aren't all you'll need to wear. If you're going to be a serious polar scientist, you'll need serious polar gear. Forget flapping about in a grubby white coat, like your barking mad science teacher – you need to wrap up warm. So what is the serious polar scientist wearing these days? Here's Gloria again with more freezing fashions.

GOGGLES: TO PROTECT YOUR EYES FROM THE SUN'S GLARE AND FROM WIND-BLOWN SNOW

THIN FLEECY TOP: WORN OVER YOUR UNDIES. FLEECE IS A FLUFFY FABRIC MADE OUT OF PLASTIC FIBRES AND IS BRILLIANTLY LIGHT AND WARM

THERMAL UNDIES: LONG JOHNS AND LONG-SLEEVED VEST WORN NEXT TO YOUR SKIN

RUCKSACK: FOR CARRYING YOUR SPARE CLOTHES AND FIRST-AID KIT

FLEECY FACE MASK AND FUR-LINED HOOD: TO STOP YOUR BREATH FREEZING ON YOUR SKIN

SALOPETTES AND JACKET: A TWO-PIECE OUTFIT FILLED WITH DOWN (A BIT LIKE WEARING YOUR DUVET). THEY'RE WINDPROOF, WATERPROOF AND WELL INSULATED, AND WILL KEEP YOU WARM AND SNUG. IT'S ALSO 'BREATHABLE'. THIS MEANS IT LETS SWEAT ESCAPE SO YOUR CLOTHES DON'T GET SODDEN AND FREEZE

GLOVES: YOU'LL NEED TWO PAIRS. WEAR A THIN PAIR OF THERMAL GLOVES UNDERNEATH WITH FLEECE-LINED MITTENS ON TOP

MUKLUKS (BOOTS): MADE FROM RUBBER WITH A CANVAS TOP, WITH THICK, RIDGED RUBBER SOLES SO YOU DON'T SLIP. IT'S BEST TO WEAR THERMAL LINERS INSIDE YOUR BOOTS AND SEVERAL PAIRS OF THICK, THERMAL SOCKS

OR YOU COULD WEAR STURDY CLIMBING BOOTS MADE FROM STRONG, LIGHT PLASTIC. STRAP CRAMPONS (METAL SPIKES) TO THE SOLES TO GET A GRIP ON THE ICE

Note: Like the horribly hardy Inuit, Antarctic scientists wear layers of clothes. These are brilliant at trapping warm air and you can take them off if you get too hot (yes, it can happen). This outfit should keep you warm even if the temperature plummets to a f-f-freezing –40°C.

HORRIBLE HEALTH WARNING

In Antarctica, it's vital to wrap up warm. Otherwise you might end up with fatal frostbite. It attacks your fingers, toes, ears and nose. First they feel prickly, then they go numb. Then they swell up and turn red. And then they go black and drop off. Horrible.

Hypothermia's another horrible hazard. Symptoms include shivering, sluggishness and slurring your words. Eventually, your body temperature drops so much you lose consciousness and can even die.

5 Easy going? You'll need to be. OK, so going to Antarctica's an amazing adventure but it does have its downside. For starters, you'll be stuck on a station for months on end, cut off from the outside world. The dark, the cold and the cramped conditions could easily get on your nerves. Not to mention your fellow suffering scientists.

Trouble is, if things get really bad, you can't just pop outside for a stroll. So you've got to stay chilled. If you get horribly homesick, you can always send an email home.

6 Good at languages? It helps. Science is full of baffling words which can be appallingly long and confusing. To muddle matters even more, polar scientists have their own secret code. I mean, what on Earth are these two talking about?

(Rough translation)
Dingle day – a beautiful day
Jolly – a fun camping trip
Smoko – a tea-break
Bog chisel – a metal stick for checking sea ice
Gash – rubbish

7 Allergic to baths? If baths bring you out in a rash, here's some great news. You can go for days without washing in Antarctica and no one will know you pong. That's because smells are made from tiny particles floating in the moist air. But you can't smell a thing in Antarctica – the air's too

91

desperately dry. Besides, if you're on a field trip, there aren't going to be any bathrooms. So if you want to go to the toilet, you'll have to dig yourself an, er, ig-loo. It's a big pit in the snow, complete with a loo seat. Don't forget to take everything with you when you leave camp. And that includes any turdicles. Yep, they're like giant icicles but you can guess what they're made from.

8 Neat and tidy? You'll need to be. Everything you need in Antarctica has to be brought by plane or ship. That means food, clothes, building materials, scientific instruments, beds, curtains – you get the picture. And you have to take all your rubbish away with you. Rubbish used to be dumped in the sea or buried under the snow. Today, it's shipped home to be recycled or burned. Otherwise, all this pollution might have a fatal effect on Antarctica's unique landscape and wildlife.

9 Growing a beard? Not essential, but it helps you to look the part. A beard will also keep your face warm, but mind it doesn't freeze. Wear a false beard if you don't have a real one.

Scientists wanted – apply now

Still keen on becoming a polar scientist? Now you've got to decide what sort of scientist you want to be. Take a peek at these pages from the special Antarctic edition of the *Daily Globe* to pick the perfect job for you.

Daily Globe | JOB HUNT

GLORIOUS OPPORTUNITIES FOR-GLACIOLOGISTS!

JOB DESCRIPTION:
If you like ice, this is the job for you. You'll spend most of your time knee deep in the stuff.

SKILLS REQUIRED:
You'll need to be able to tell how old ice is by drilling out ice cores and studying them (see pages 47-48), using high-tech equipment.

WE'LL PROVIDE:
radars and satellites to help you work out how much ice there is, and how fast it's melting.

BRILLIANT BASE FOR-BIOLOGISTS!

JOB DESCRIPTION:
You'll enjoy studying how living things survive at the Poles, without freezing to death.

SKILLS REQUIRED:
Must be prepared to tackle everything from tracking albatrosses by satellite to scuba diving under the frozen sea to follow fish and seals.

WE'LL PROVIDE:
equipment for drilling miles and miles down through the ice to study bacteria recently discovered in ancient lakes. We need someone to work out how they got there…

MUST HAVE - METEOROLOGISTS!

JOB DESCRIPTION: You'll love braving the bone-chilling cold to find out all about the polar weather, and forecast the weather around the world.

SKILLS REQUIRED: You'll need to be a whizz at maths. There's lots of checking equipment and long sums involved.

WE'LL PROVIDE: satellite equipment, so you can monitor the size of the hole in the ozone layer, recently discovered by polar scientists. (See Poles in Peril for the hole, sorry whole story.) We'll also provide automatic weather stations.

Great jobs for go-ahead-GEOLOGISTS!

JOB DESCRIPTION: You'll be able to find out about the Earth by looking at rotten rocks. After tracking the rocks down, that is. You'll also study how glaciers grind rocks down.

SKILLS REQUIRED: As you know, most of the land in Antarctica's buried under ice. You'll also need an eye for precious metals – there are small amounts of gold, silver and other metals hidden in some of the rocks. You'll also study volcanoes – hope you're feeling brave. In 1969, a volcano on Deception Island blew its top, destroying two nearby scientific stations.

WE'LL PROVIDE: radar and satellites for you to peek at the peaks underneath.

PERFECT POSITIONS FOR PALAEONTOLOGISTS!

JOB DESCRIPTION:

You'll love studying fossils in the rocks to find out what life was like long ago. You might find fossils of plants, reptiles and even long-dead dinosaurs.

SKILLS REQUIRED:

You'll be able to compare crucial fossil clues with similar fossils found in other parts of the world, to unearth the history of the polar regions. Worth knowing that scientists have already worked out that Antarctica was once toasty and warm, and part of a massive supercontinent. (See page 33 for the heart-warming details.)

WE'LL PROVIDE:

tools for getting the fossils and transport for lugging them home (so you won't have to drag a sledge full of rocks like Captain Scott and his men).

ASTOUNDING ADVENTURES FOR ASTRONOMERS!

JOB DESCRIPTION:

You'll be tracking the sun with telescopes, along with other stars and planets. You'll also be on the lookout for masses of meteorites (lumps of space rock), lying around on the ice.

SKILLS REQUIRED:

Must be able to handle other excited astronomers who've recently found loads of meteorites. They believe that the rocks are millions of years old and come from the moon and from Mars. Astronomers also study the aurorae (see page 34) and space weather (rays from outer space which reach the Earth). Space storms can knock out satellites, cause power black-outs and be desperately dangerous for astronauts on space walks from the space shuttle.

WE'LL PROVIDE:

incredibly clear air to make your job as easy as pie and, in summer, all-day sunshine. So keeping track of the sun will be a breeze.

So, you're armed with your new-found knowledge of the perishing Poles. You think you've found your ideal job and you've packed your false beard. But, hang on a minute, before you get too big for your sealskin boots, spare a thought for those plucky polar pioneers who didn't make the grade. For years, intrepid explorers have set off to find out what the fuss was all about. Only some of them lived to tell the teeth-chattering tale…

Some people like skating on very thin ice. Or sailing close to the wind. A nice, quiet life in front of the telly would bore them to tears. Nope, they want excitement and adventure. And they'll go to the ends of the Earth for it. Despite the dreadful dangers, people have been exploring the perishing Poles for years. They've braved icebergs, blizzards and polar bears. But what on Earth did they do it for? Some of them were in it for money. They wanted to open the Poles up for trade. Others simply wanted to see bits of the world no one had ever seen before. Besides, being a polar explorer was seen as a dead glamorous job. Fame and fortune were guaranteed. If you made it back alive, that is.

Early explorers

First reports from the far north

In about 325 BC, a globe-trotting Greek, Pytheas, set sail on an astonishing voyage. He spent years sailing across the North Atlantic and exploring the frozen north. He even got as far as Iceland, or so he said. Sadly, when he finally got back home again, nobody believed him. You could say they gave poor Pytheas the cold shoulder. People laughed when he said he'd seen seas covered in ice that shook like wobbly jelly. A likely tale, they said. (In fact, geographers now know this was pancake ice.)

WAS THERE CUSTARD AS WELL ?

And they sniggered at his description of a place where the sun shone all night in summer but didn't rise in winter. (They'd never heard of the midnight sun, you see.) Pytheas spent the rest of his life trying to convince people he wasn't fibbing.

Adventurous Vikings

But it was really the adventurous Vikings who put the Arctic on the map. In about AD 982, a vicious Viking called Erik the Red went to live in Greenland. (He had to flee from Iceland where he was wanted for a bloody murder.) Of course, it wasn't called Greenland then. Enterprising Erik made up the name to trick other Vikings into going with him. And guess what? It worked a treat. Greenland sounded so, well, er, green, that people happily packed up and went. Goodness knows what they thought when they got there, faced with freezing cold weather and awesome icebergs.

GREENLAND

IF IT'S NOT GREEN, IT'S NOT HERE!

SCANDINAVIAN TOURIST BOARD AD 982

Despite the hostile conditions, the hardy Vikings flourished for almost 500 years. They farmed the land and kept sheep, goats and cattle. Gradually, they disappeared – no one knows why. Some people think they were kidnapped by pirates or died from the plague. But experts reckon there was a sudden cold snap and the Vikings froze to death. Trouble is, their clothes weren't warm enough and they didn't know how to hunt for food. So when the cold weather killed their crops, the unlucky Vikings starved. If only they'd asked the local people for some life-saving survival tips.

Into the unknown
Meanwhile, at the other end of the Earth, Antarctica was still a mystery, even though the ancient Greeks guessed it was there. On early maps, it was labelled *Terra Australis Incognita*, which means "unknown southern land". But no one had ever been there.

Then, in 1772, go-getting English explorer, Captain James Cook (1728-1779), sailed off in search of the fabled continent. James didn't actually see it but he crossed the

Antarctic Circle for the first time and sailed right round Antarctica before pack ice forced him back. Bitterly disappointed, Cook wrote glumly in his diary:

The greater part of such a continent must lie within the Polar Circle, where the sea is so pestered with ice that the land is inaccessible. Thick fogs, snow storms, intense cold ... are heightened by the inexpressibly horrid aspect of the country, doomed by nature to lie buried under everlasting ice and snow.

As far as he was concerned, he added gloomily, Antarctica was of no use to anyone.

In fact, the first person to set foot on Antarctica was probably an American, John Davis. He landed in February 1821 to hunt for seals. And that sealed his fate, you could say.

Earth-shattering fact

When Captain Cook died, his friends put on a pantomime in London to celebrate his globe-trotting life. But forget boring pantomime horses. In honour of Cook's Antarctic adventures, a specially made mini iceberg stole the show.

AND NOW FOR MY FIRST TRICK

Teacher teaser

Everyone knows that Amundsen reached the South Pole first but what about the nippy North Pole? Test your teacher's polar know-how with this harmless-sounding question. Stick up your hand and say:

PLEASE, MISS, WHO REACHED THE NORTH POLE FIRST?

ER...ER...

Answer: Sorry, this is a trick question. You see, the answer depends on whose story you believe. While your teacher's making her mind up, we've dug out an old copy of the *Daily Globe* to fill you in on the real-life details...

The Daily Globe

NEW YORK, USA

TOP EXPLORERS IN POLAR PUNCH-UP

Bitter controversy raged today as not one but two of our best-known explorers claimed the honour of being the first person at the North Pole. Yesterday, we received the sensational news that Commander Robert Peary of the US Navy had braved frostbite and biting blizzards to conquer the North Pole. He reached the Pole on 6 April. For Peary, 53, it was a dream come true and this doughty polar veteran was understandably thrilled.

"My life's work is accomplished," he told our reporter. "I have got the North Pole out of my system after 23 years of effort, hard work, disappointments, hardships, privations, more or less suffering, and some risks. I have won the last great geographical prize, the North Pole, for the credit of the United States… I am content."

With two failed attempts behind him, it was third time lucky for plucky Peary. He put his success down to months spent learning essential Inuit survival skills. At the Pole, Peary and his companions hoisted an American flag and posed for a photo.

PEARY'S POLE

The flag was made by Peary's wife, Josephine.

PROUD MOMENT

"The bitter wind burned our faces so that they cracked," Commander Peary told us. "The air was keen and bitter as frozen steel."

A heroic feat indeed.

Or was it? No sooner had the news broken than the story took an extraordinary turn. As Peary's news reached home, his bitter rival, Dr Frederick Cook was celebrating his discovery of the North Pole at a banquet in Copenhagen. A one-time travelling companion of Peary, Dr Cook has just returned from a two-year expedition to the Arctic. Incredibly, he claims to have reached the Pole on 21 April 1908, a whole year before Peary.

JUST WHAT THE DOCTOR ORDERED

When Cook was told of Peary's achievement, he replied graciously. "If he has announced he has reached the farthest North, he has," Cook said. "There is honour enough on it for both of us."

The question is: which of these two intrepid explorers is telling the truth. Who should we believe? Will it be proud Peary or courageous Cook who claims his place in history? The story looks set to run and run. *The Daily Globe* will keep you up-to-date with all the latest developments.

In pole position

When Peary heard Cook's claim, he was furious. You can understand why. He called Cook a liar and vowed to find out the truth. Unluckily for Peary, the public were on Cook's side. Cheering crowds welcomed him home with "WE BELIEVE YOU!" banners.

Both men had their diaries and notebooks examined by learned geographical societies who eventually ruled in Peary's favour, even though there wasn't any real proof. Trouble is, Cook's dates didn't add up, they said. And the piece of land he claimed to have seen didn't actually exist. Worse still, crafty Cook has already been proved a fibber. A few years before, he claimed to have climbed Mount McKinley in Alaska (the highest peak in North America) for the first time. In fact, his photos later turned out to be fakes. Cook was expelled from the Explorers' Club of New York and spent the rest of his life in disgrace.

So was Peary telling the truth? It was difficult to tell. Some people reckoned he'd made it all up. After all, they said, there was no way he could have got to the Pole and back as quickly as he claimed.

Who do you believe?

P-p-p-pick your own polar explorer

Picture the scene. You're stranded at the perishing Poles and you're allowed one person to keep you company. But who should you choose? They'll need to be brave, tough and determined, and ice-cool in an emergency. Each of the polar pioneers below have proved they're intrepid explorers. All you have to do is pick the one you think's the pluckiest. Here's Gloria to introduce our five daring contestants...

Each of our contestants has already pitted their survival skills against the perishing Poles. But now it's your turn to choose one of them to be your travelling companion. Make sure you're equipped for the trip of a lifetime by listening carefully to their case histories before you choose...

POLE PEOPLE

Contestant no. 1
NAME: Willem Barents (1550?-1597)
NATIONALITY: Dutch
CLAIM TO FAME: Brave Barents made three daring voyages in search of a new sea route to Asia across the north of Siberia. When his ship got stuck in the ice, he became the first European to spend winter in the freezing Arctic. Brrrr!
SPECIAL SKILLS: Building a house out of a shipwreck. To pick weather-beaten Willem, vote for contestant number 1.

Contestant no. 2
NAME: Sir John Franklin (1786-1847)
NATIONALITY: British
CLAIM TO FAME: Salty old sea dog, Sir John had travelled the world. He spent years sailing in the Arctic in search of a new sea route to Asia across the north of Canada. OK, so he didn't find it but he got his own statue in Westminster Abbey in London. So there.
SPECIAL SKILLS: A brilliant navigator and sailor.
To pick seaworthy Sir John, vote for contestant number 2.

Contestant no. 3
NAME: Salomon Andrée (1854-1897)
NATIONALITY: Swedish
CLAIM TO FAME: Attempted to become the first person to fly to the North Pole in a hot-air balloon. The balloon was called the Eagle. Salomon was so famous he had his waxwork displayed at Madame Tussaud's in London. Now that's cool!
SPECIAL SKILLS: Mad about flying.
To pick high-flying Salomon, vote for contestant number 3.

Contestant no. 4
NAME: Knud Rasmussen (1879–1933)
NATIONALITY: Danish/Inuit
CLAIM TO FAME: Clever Knud was the first person to study how the Inuit people lived and survived in the icy Arctic. They taught Knud everything he knew and he became a top polar expert.
SPECIAL SKILLS: Hunting, fishing, driving dog sledges.
To pick knowledgeable Knud, vote for contestant number 4.

Contestant no. 5
NAME: Sir Douglas Mawson (1882–1958)
NATIONALITY: Australian
CLAIM TO FAME: Brilliant scientist Sir Douglas led the Australasian Antarctic Expedition in 1911. He explored an unknown stretch of coast and found the first Antarctic meteorite.
SPECIAL SKILLS: Toughness and determination.
To pick daring Sir Douglas, vote for contestant number 5.

So which of these cool customers did you choose? You're about to find out if you'll survive the journey. Here are the results in reverse order...

5 If you chose contestant number 2, you're lost. Hopelessly lost. Sir John might have been brilliant at navigating at sea but on land it was another story. In 1845, Sir John set sail for the Arctic with 128 men. And was never heard from again. His worried wife offered a £20,000 reward (a fortune in those days) and sent out several search parties. Her husband was nowhere to be found. Finally, in 1859, the searchers found a note hidden under a pile of stones. It said daring Sir John had died in 1847, trying to fetch help.

4 If you chose contestant number 3, you'll survive but only for three months. In 1897, Salomon and two companions took off from Spitsbergen in Norway to fly to the North Pole. But just three days after take-off, the balloon got weighed down with ice and was forced to crash-land. The three men survived for three months on a diet of polar bear meat. But, sadly, all three perished. It was only in 1930 that their bodies were finally found and their tragic story pieced together from their diaries and photos. (To make matters worse, Salomon's waxwork was eaten by mice.)

3 If you chose contestant number 1, you'll be OK, but you might have trouble getting back. Worthy Willem was cool as a cucumber in a crisis, and horribly practical, too. When his ship got stuck, did he panic? Did he, heck! He coolly built a cosy hut on the ice, out of the ship's timbers. It even had a bath tub, made out of an old wine cask. And instead of hot-water bottles, the men took hot stones to bed instead. Unfortunately, Willem didn't make it back. In summer, he tried to sail for home but died from scurvy. (Though most of his men survived.)

2 If you chose contestant number 4, you'll be in safe hands, though you might die from food poisoning. Cool Knud grew up in Greenland. As a kid, he learned how to hunt, fish and drive a dog sledge like an Inuit. He could also speak several Inuit languages. What a swot! Knud later went to Denmark to train as an opera singer. But he was soon back in Greenland where he set up a bank instead. He used the money he made from banking to fund more expeditions. (Knud eventually died from food poisoning caused by eating a bad pickled auk.)

But the winner is ... Contestant number 5. You'll definitely survive with fearless Douglas. In fact, he'll probably outlast you. Gutsy Sir Douglas Mawson showed just how to survive against all the odds. While out on a sledging trip, one of his companions suddenly disappeared down a crevasse, taking his sledge, dogs, tent and all their food down with him. Then his other companion died from food poisoning (by this time, they'd been forced to eat the rest of the dogs). Half-dead himself, Sir Douglas struggled on alone. Somehow he made it back to camp ... just in time to see his ship sailing away! He was forced to spend another winter in Antarctica. Congratulations, Sir Douglas! Talk about keeping your cool.

HI MUM!

So congratulations to those of you who picked our worthy winner. Your special prize is a thrilling dog sledge ride to the North Pole. Yes, you'll soon be hurtling across the ice at full speed ... pulled by a pack of pooches! Don't panic. They're brilliant at spotting crevasses (usually). Just one thing before you set off. We've left it to you to set the sledge up.

Drive a dog sledge

What you need:
- a wooden sledge
- about five to ten huskies

What you do:

1 Round up your huskies. Huskies are horribly hardy dogs, perfectly suited to polar travel. (They also make brilliant pets – if you can get them off your sofa.) They've got thick, woolly coats to keep them warm, and they're super-strong (a team of ten huskies can pull you and a fully loaded sledge 50 kilometres a day).

And you can feed huskies on seal blubber if you've forgotten to bring the tin opener. (By the way, they go to sleep curled up in the snow, so there's no need for a dog kennel.)

2 Hitch your huskies to your sledge, in a fan formation. Each dog has a specially padded harness which goes round its chest (not round its neck like an ordinary dog collar). Fix them to the sledge by nylon ropes called traces. Let the strongest, most intelligent dog take the lead. The traces spread out in a fan shape. So if the lead dog falls into a crevasse, the others won't follow (you hope).

3 Stand on the back of the sledge. Call "*Hike! Hike!*" – that's the command to get the dogs moving. (Other useful commands include: *Gee* – turn right; *Haw* – turn left; *Straight on* – go straight; *Easy* – slow down; *Whoa* – stop; and *On-by* – put that rabbit down.)

Now you're really mushing (that's the technical term for driving a dog sledge).

(Important note: to brake, stand on the metal bar between the sledge runners and push it down into the snow.)

4 If your dogs get tired (should that be dog tired?), you'll need to pedal the sledge yourself. That means pushing the sledge forward with one foot, as if you're riding a scooter. Don't worry if you keep falling off – mushing takes years of practice. But once you get the hang of it, it's a horribly thrilling ride. *Hike! Hike!*

Note: You can't go mushing in Antarctica. Since 1994, dogs have been banned. Scientists thought they had distemper (a deadly disease) and might spread it to the seals.

Modern-day exploration

If all this talk of adventure has given you itchy feet, why not explore the perishing poles yourself? Each year, hundreds of people set off for the poles. But if mushing isn't your cup of tea, there are lots of other exciting ways of getting about. You could hitch a lift on an aeroplane (many polar planes have skis instead of wheels so they can land safely on the ice) or take a cruise in an icebreaker (a specially strengthened steel ship for smashing through the ice). You could even go by submarine. In 1958, an American sub, *Nautilus*, reached the North Pole by travelling all the way under the ice.

Unlike explorers of the past, modern explorers have lots of mod cons to help them. They use radios and email to keep in touch and satellites to help them navigate. Even then, exploring the perishing Poles is a horribly risky thing to do. With day-long darkness and white-outs, it's easy to get hoplessly lost. Dead lost. After a while, one ice floe looks much the same as another and there aren't any handy road signs around. If this happens, you might like to take a leaf out of the local Inuits' book. They use the sun or the pattern made by the wind in the snow to help them find their way. Whatever you do, never fix your route from an iceberg. It'll keep drifting off to sea...

POLES IN PERIL

But apart from exploring, what on Earth can you use a perishing Pole for? I mean, the Poles are just piles of useless old ice stuck miles away from anywhere, aren't they? Wrong. Hidden under the ice and the frozen seas are some really useful polar riches. Trouble is, horrible humans are so busy trying to get them out that they're putting the fragile Poles at risk. So why are the Poles in peril? Here are five precious polar prizes and how horrible humans might be spoiling them.

Polar prize 1: Fabulous fur seals

What we're doing: In the 18th and 19th centuries in Antarctica, millions of seals were killed for their fur. It was used to make fancy fur hats, coats, slippers and felt cloth for fashionable ladies in Europe, America and China.

Elephant seals were also clobbered to death for their blubber (which was boiled down to make high-quality oil) and walruses were killed for their ivory.

What's wrong with that? So many seals were slaughtered that some species were almost wiped out. Pretty grim, eh? The good news is, large-scale hunting of some seals is now completely banned, though local people can still catch a few for food. Since the hunting stopped, seal stocks have quickly recovered and the seals are now protected.

Polar prize 2: Whopping whales

What we're doing: And it wasn't just the seals the hunters were after. Millions of whales were killed for their meat, blubber and whalebone. It was used for making combs, fishing rods, umbrellas and posh ladies' corsets. Even 100 years ago a whalebone from a large-ish whale could fetch a whopping £2,500. Whale hunting was big business.

What's wrong with that? At one time, whales were hunted almost to extinction. And they're still pretty rare. Today, though, there are strict rules to protect the whales from harm. A few hundred whales can be killed each year for food or scientific research. But commercial hunting is banned. In 1994, Antarctica and the Southern Ocean were officially declared a Whale Sanctuary. And whopping whales are making a come-back.

Polar prize 3: Deep-freeze fish

What we're doing: Fishing fleets catch million of tonnes of fish, krill and squid each year from polar seas. Modern trawlers are horribly high-tech. They use computers, radar and satellites to track the seafood down, and enormous nets to catch it. Some are like floating fish factories. They can clean, freeze and can fish on board. Handy, eh?

What's wrong with that? Some fishermen are breaking the rules about how many fish they can catch. That's bad luck for Patagonian toothfish. Their tasty meat makes them a very valuable catch. Trouble is, it takes a toothfish about 30 years to reach adult size (about 2 metres). And so many fish are being caught (illegally), they don't have time to catch up. To make matters worse, thousands of seabirds, like albatrosses, get tangled up in the fishing lines.

Polar prize 4: Oodles of oil

What we're doing: There's oodles of precious oil under the Arctic ice and tundra. And horrible humans are digging deep to get it out. Serious supplies of oil have already been found in icy Siberia and Alaska. It's pumped out of the ground and piped thousands of miles to an oil refinery.

So what's wrong with that? Well, the roads and pipes lines used to transport the oil are spoiling the fragile polar habitat. Take the plight of the Arctic National Wildlife Refuge in Alaska. It's the largest national park in the USA but it may soon be history. That's if the US government goes ahead with its plans to drill for oil. Then there's the risk of oil spills. In 1989, the oil tanker, *Exxon Valdez*, ran aground off the coast of Alaska, spilling 50 million litres of oil into the sea. That's enough to fill 13 Olympic-sized swimming pools.

And that's an awful lot of oil. A huge stretch of coast was soaked in oil, and thousands of fish, birds and sea mammals were killed. There may be loads of oil off the Antarctic coast, too, but it's horribly hard to find. Besides, commercial mining of any sort is banned in Antarctica until at least the year 2041.

Polar prize 5: Horrible holidays
What we're doing: Every year, thousands of tourists head for the perishing Poles. Believe it or not. Fancy a horrible holiday?

Horrible Holidays
are proud to present their

PERISHING POLAR ☆ CRUISE ☆

FED UP WITH LOUNGING ABOUT ON THE BEACH?

TIRED OF BORING DAYS OUT AT THE ZOO?

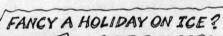

FANCY A HOLIDAY ON ICE?

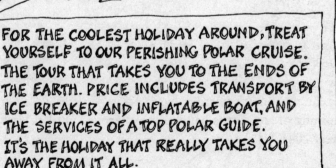

BOOK NOW   PLACES LIMITED

FOR THE COOLEST HOLIDAY AROUND, TREAT
YOURSELF TO OUR PERISHING POLAR CRUISE.
THE TOUR THAT TAKES YOU TO THE ENDS OF
THE EARTH. PRICE INCLUDES TRANSPORT BY
ICE BREAKER AND INFLATABLE BOAT, AND
THE SERVICES OF A TOP POLAR GUIDE.
IT'S THE HOLIDAY THAT REALLY TAKES YOU
AWAY FROM IT ALL.

SMALL PRINT.

DON'T FORGET TO BRING A GOOD BOOK. IF THE WEATHER'S BAD YOU
MIGHT BE STUCK ON BOARD FOR DAYS ON END. AND THERE'S ONLY SO
MANY SHOTS OF ICEBERGS YOU CAN SNAP AND TAKE HOME TO
BORE YOUR FRIENDS WITH.

What's wrong with that? Some people think tourists might be doing more harm than good. Especially if they disturb the local wildlife and leave loads of litter behind. On the other hand, if they go home and tell other people how amazingly cool the perishing Poles can be, it might help to save them.

If you're heading for Antarctica on holiday, here are some simple dos and don'ts for keeping the Poles in peak condition.

DO...
• Keep your distance from the birds and seals. Especially when you're taking their piccy. If they notice you, you're too close. Never feed or touch them.
• Take all your litter home with you. Don't chuck anything overboard from your cruise ship.
• Check with any research station before you pay them a visit. You might get in the scientists' way.

120

DON'T...

• Walk on any lichens, mosses or flowers. They're horribly delicate and will take years to grow back again.

• Collect any rocks, fossils or bones as souvenirs.

• Wander off on your own – Antarctica's a perilous place. Stick with your group and keep to set tracks and trails and listen to instructions from your polar guide.

• Walk on glacier or snow fields. You might not spot a lethal crevasse until it's too late.

• Shout! You'll frighten the animals – they're used to peace and quiet.

121

HORRIBLE HEALTH WARNING

In the early 1980s, scientists discovered a huge hole in the ozone layer above the South Pole. Ozone's a horribly useful gas that blocks out the sun's burning ultraviolet rays. Too much of these and you'd be burned to a crisp. Very nasty. And the hole's growing every year. In fact, it's now about twice the size of the hole, sorry, whole, of Europe.

Guess who was to blame? Yep, horrible humans, of course. For years, we'd been dumping tonnes of ghastly gases called CFCs (chlorofluorocarbons) into the atmosphere. They were used in fridges, foam and aerosol sprays (like spray-on deodorants).

Luckily, we're cleaning up our act and CFCs have been banned. (By the way, this doesn't mean you have to pong. These days most deodorants are CFC-free.) But CFCs take a long time to disappear from the atmosphere. It will take at least 50 years for the ozone hole to mend.

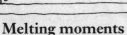

Melting moments

But if you really fancy a holiday on ice, you'd better get your skates on. What's the rush? Well, horrible geographers are worried that the perishing Poles are melting because the Earth's getting warmer. Already, huge chunks of ice are breaking off Antarctica, and the Arctic sea ice is shrinking. The question is: are humans to blame this time or is it down to nasty nature? Time to call the experts in. The only problem is finding two horrible geographers that agree – about anything!

It's people who are to blame, I'm afraid. We're pumping too many ghastly greenhouse gases* into the atmosphere. And they're making the world warm up at an alarming rate.

* They're gases like carbon dioxide and methane that keep the Earth snug and warm. They work a bit like the glass in your grandad's greenhouse – they let the sun's rays in but stop heat from the Earth escaping. These gases come from exhaust fumes from cars and lorries, pollution from factories and power stations, and from burning too many rainforest trees.

Stuff and nonsense. It's nature to blame. The Earth's climate changes naturally. It never stays the same for long. After all, we've been having cold snaps and warm spells for millions of years.

Even so, most scientists now reckon that horrible humans are to blame for our warming world. They predict that the Earth will heat up by about 2°C by the year 2100. Which might not sound much to you but just a teeny rise in temperature could melt the ice sheets and glaciers at the Poles. If this happened, an awesome amount of water would pour into the sea, raising sea level by 50 metres or more, and drowning many low-lying islands and cities. Watch out if you live in London or Venice - it's going to get horribly soggy.

A PERISHING FUTURE?

So what does the future hold for the perishing Poles? Is it all gloom and doom? The good news is that people are working hard to keep the Poles pristine.

A tricky treaty

At the North Pole, the land is owned by the various Arctic nations. But who owns the South Pole? The answer is: nobody. In 1959, 12 countries signed a historic document called the Antarctic Treaty. It sets out how Antarctica is governed. These countries promised to make sure Antarctica is protected and is used for peaceful purposes only. And the good news is, so far the Treaty seems to be working. Today, 44 countries have signed up. Here's what they've agreed to do:

- To make Antarctica a natural reserve devoted to peace and science
- To allow scientists freedom to work
- To share scientific know-how
- To set aside any territorial claims
- To ban nuclear explosions and the disposal of radioactive waste
- To meet every year and agree new ways to protect the continent

In 1998, another bit was added to the Antarctic Treaty. It bans any mining or drilling for oil in Antarctica, and protects Antarctica's unique wildlife. It also says that scientists and tourists must take all their waste away with them, in case it harms the fragile environment. Will this be enough to protect the Pole? We'll just have to wait and see. Some people say that the only way to save the Pole for good is to turn Antarctica into a giant World Park. But they're still arguing about who'd be the park keeper. In the meantime, one thing's for certain. The perishing Poles are amazing wildernesses, with people and animals found nowhere else on Earth. It would be a terrible tragedy if they disappeared. Besides, they're the coolest places on the planet to be. And that's the teeth–chattering truth.

Websites

If you're still interested in finding out more, here are some polar websites you can check out:

www.antarctica.ac.uk
The British Antarctic Survey's website, with up-to-date info and diaries of scientists based in Antarctica.

www.spri.cam.ac.uk
The Scott Polar Research Institute. Info about Arctic people, explorers, landscape and wildlife.

www.south-pole.com
Masses of info about Antarctic explorers, and facts and figures about polar weather.

www.glacier.rice.edu
Maps, lists, facts and figures about conditions at the North and South Poles.

www.heritage-antarctica.org
The website of the Antarctic Heritage Trust. Join the trust and help save Scott and Shackleton's old expedition huts (you'll also get a copy of its newsletter, *Bergy Bits*).

www.iaato.org
The website of the International Association of Antarctica Tour Operators has information about Antarctic tourism.

http://bat.phys.unsw.edu.au/~aasto
Check out the AASTO (Automated Astrophysical Site-Testing Observatory) webcam at the South Pole.

www.survival-international.org
Survival International's website. Survival is a worldwide organization helping local people protect their homes and land. Contact them for a copy of their brilliant pack "We, the world". It includes info about the lives of the Chukchi and other Arctic people.